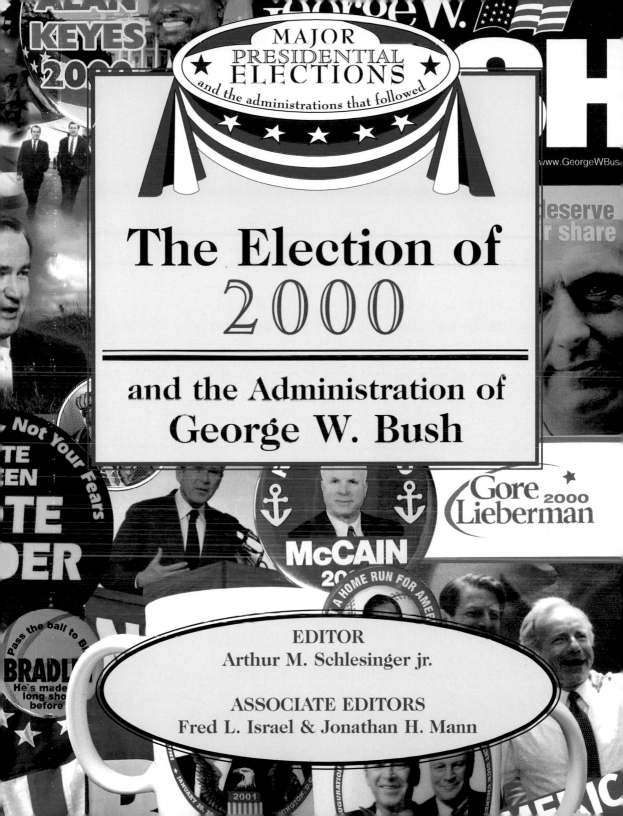

MAJOR
PRESIDENTIAL
ELECTIONS
and the administrations that followed

The Election of
2000

and the Administration of
George W. Bush

EDITOR
Arthur M. Schlesinger jr.

ASSOCIATE EDITORS
Fred L. Israel & Jonathan H. Mann

MAJOR
PRESIDENTIAL
ELECTIONS
and the administrations that followed

The Election of
2000

and the Administration of George W. Bush

EDITOR

Arthur M. Schlesinger, jr.
Albert Schweitzer Chair in the Humanities
The City University of New York

ASSOCIATE EDITORS

Fred L. Israel
Department of History
The City College of New York

Jonathan H. Mann
Publisher
The Rail Splitter

Mason Crest Publishers
Philadelphia

Produced by OTTN Publishing, Stockton, New Jersey

Mason Crest Publishers
370 Reed Road
Broomall PA 19008
www.masoncrest.com

Research Consultant: Patrick R. Hilferty
Editorial Assistant: Jane Ziff

First printing

1 3 5 7 9 8 6 4 2

Library of Congress Cataloging-in-Publication Data

The election of 2000 and the administration of George W. Bush / editor, Arthur M.
Schlesinger, Jr. ; associate editors, Fred L. Israel & Jonathan H. Mann.
    p. cm. — (Major presidential elections and the administrations that followed)
Summary: A discussion of the presidential election of 2000 and the subsequent administration
of George W. Bush, based on source documents.
    Includes bibliographical references and index.
    ISBN 1-59084-365-7
1. Presidents—United States—Election—2000—Juvenile literature. 2. Presidents—United
States—Election—2000—Sources—Juvenile literature 3. Bush, George W. (George Walker),
1946-   —Juvenile literature. 4. United States—Politics and government—2001-   —Juvenile
literature. 5. United States—Politics and government—2001-   —Sources—Juvenile literature.
[1. Presidents—Election—2000—Sources. 2. Bush, George W. (George Walker), 1946-
3. Elections. 4. United States—Politics and government—2001-   —Sources.] I. Schlesinger,
Arthur Meier, 1917-   II. Israel, Fred L. III. Mann, Jonathan H. IV. Series.
E889 .E44 2002
324.973'0929—dc21

2002013397

Publisher's note: all quotations in this book come
from original sources, and contain the spelling and
grammatical inconsistencies of the original text.

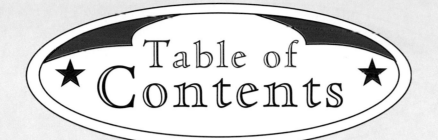

Table of Contents

America suffers from a sort of intermittent fever—what one may call a quintan ague. Every fourth year there come terrible shakings, passing into the hot fit of the presidential election; then follows what physicians call "the interval"; then again the fit.

—James Bryce, The American Commonwealth (1888)

Running for president is the central rite in the American political order. It was not always so. *Choosing* the chief magistrate had been the point of the quadrennial election from the beginning, but it took a long while for candidates to *run* for the highest office in the land; that is, to solicit, visibly and actively, the support of the voters. These volumes show through text and illustration how those aspiring to the White House have moved on from ascetic self-restraint to shameless self-merchandising. This work thereby illuminates the changing ways the American people have conceived the role of their President. I hope it will also recall to new generations some of the more picturesque and endearing dimensions of American politics.

The primary force behind the revolution in campaign attitudes and techniques was a development unforeseen by the men who framed the Constitution—the rise of the party system. Party competition was not at all their original intent. Quite the contrary: inspired at one or two removes by Lord Bolingbroke's British tract of half a century earlier, *The Idea of a Patriot King*, the Founding Fathers envisaged a Patriot President, standing above party and faction, representing the whole people, offering the nation non-partisan leadership virtuously dedicated to the common good.

The ideal of the Patriot President was endangered, the Founding Fathers believed, by twin menaces—factionalism and factionalism's ugly offspring, the demagogue. Party competition would only encourage unscrupulous men to appeal to popular passion and prejudice. Alexander Hamilton in the 71st Federalist bemoaned the plight of the people, "beset as they continually are . . . by the snares of the ambitious, the avaricious, the desperate, by the artifices of men who possess their confidence more than they deserve it, and of those who seek to possess rather than to deserve it."

Pervading the Federalist was a theme sounded explicitly both in the first paper and the last: the fear that unleashing popular passions would bring on "the military despotism of a victorious demagogue." If the "mischiefs of faction" were, James Madison admitted in the Tenth Federalist, "sown in the nature of man," the object of politics was to repress this insidious disposition, not to yield to it. "If I could not go to heaven but with a party," said Thomas Jefferson, "I would not go there at all."

So the Father of his Country in his Farewell Address solemnly warned his countrymen against "the baneful effects of the spirit of party." That spirit, Washington conceded, was "inseparable from our nature"; but for popular government it was "truly their worst enemy." The "alternate domination of one faction over another," Washington said, would lead in the end to "formal and permanent despotism." The spirit of a party, "a fire not to be quenched . . . demands a uniform vigilance to prevent its bursting into a flame, lest, instead of warming, it should consume."

Yet even as Washington called on Americans to "discourage and restrain" the spirit of party, parties were beginning to crystallize around him. The eruption of partisanship in defiance of such august counsel argued that party competition might well serve functional necessities in the democratic republic.

After all, honest disagreement over policy and principle called for candid debate. And parties, it appeared, had vital roles to play in the consummation of the Constitution. The distribution of powers among three equal branches inclined the national government toward a chronic condition of stalemate. Parties offered the means of overcoming the constitutional separation of powers by coordinating the executive and legislative branches and furnishing the connective tissue essential to effective government. As national associations, moreover, parties were a force against provincialism and separatism. As instruments of compromise, they encouraged, within the parties as well as between them, the containment and mediation of national quarrels, at least until slavery broke the parties up. Henry D. Thoreau cared little enough for politics, but he saw the point: "Politics is, as it were, the gizzard of society, full of grit and gravel, and the two political parties are its two opposite halves, which grind on each other."

Furthermore, as the illustrations in these volumes so gloriously remind us, party competition was a great source of entertainment and fun—all the more important in those faraway days before the advent of baseball and football, of movies and radio and television. "To take a hand in the regulation of society and to discuss it," Alexis de Tocqueville observed when he visited America in the 1830s, "is his biggest concern and, so to speak, the only pleasure an American knows. . . . Even the women frequently attend public meetings and listen to political harangues as a recreation from their household labors. Debating clubs are, to a certain extent, a substitute for theatrical entertainments."

Condemned by the Founding Fathers, unknown to the Constitution, parties nonetheless imperiously forced themselves into political life. But the party system rose from the bottom up. For half a century, the first half-dozen Presidents continued to hold themselves above party. The disappearance of the Federalist Party after the War of 1812 suspended party competition. James Monroe, with no opponent at all in the election of 1820, presided proudly over the Era of Good Feelings, so called because there were no parties around to excite ill feelings. Monroe's successor, John Quincy Adams, despised electioneering and inveighed against the "fashion of peddling for popularity by traveling around the country gathering crowds together, hawking for public dinners, and spouting empty speeches." Men of the old republic believed presidential candidates should be men who already deserved the people's confidence rather than those seeking to win it. Character and virtue, not charisma and ambition, should be the grounds for choosing a President.

Adams was the last of the old school. Andrew Jackson, by beating him in the 1828 election, legitimized party politics and opened a new political era. The rationale of the new school was provided by Jackson's counselor and successor, Martin Van Buren, the classic philosopher of the role of party in the American democracy. By the time Van Buren took his own oath of office in 1837, parties were entrenched as the instruments of American self-government. In Van Buren's words, party battles "rouse the sluggish to exertion, give increased energy to the most active intellect, excite a salutary vigilance over our public functionaries, and prevent that apathy which has proved the ruin of Republics."

Apathy may indeed have proved the ruin of republics, but rousing the sluggish to exertion proved, ironically, the ruin of Van Buren. The architect of the party system became the first casualty of the razzle-dazzle campaigning the system quickly generated. The Whigs' Tippecanoe-and-Tyler-too campaign of 1840 transmuted the democratic Van Buren into a gilded aristocrat and assured his defeat at the polls. The "peddling for popularity" John Quincy Adams had deplored now became standard for party campaigners.

But the new methods were still forbidden to the presidential candidates themselves. The feeling lingered from earlier days that stumping the country in search of votes was demagoguery beneath the dignity of the presidency. Van Buren's code permitted—indeed expected—parties to inscribe their creed in platforms and candidates to declare their principles in letters published in newspapers. Occasionally candidates—William Henry Harrison in 1840, Winfield Scott in 1852—made a speech, but party surrogates did most of the hard work.

As late as 1858, Van Buren, advising his son John, one of the great popular orators of the time, on the best way to make it to the White House, emphasized the "rule . . . that the people will never make a man President who is so importunate as to show by his life and conversation that he not only has an eye on, but is in active pursuit of the office. . . . No man who has laid himself out for it, and was unwise enough to let the people into his secret, ever yet obtained it. Clay, Calhoun, Webster, Scott, and a host of lesser lights, should serve as a guide-post to future aspirants."

The continuing constraint on personal campaigning by candidates was reinforced by the desire of party managers to present their nominees as all things to all men. In 1835 Nicholas Biddle, the wealthy Philadelphian who had been Jackson's mortal opponent in the famous Bank War, advised the Whigs not to let General Harrison "say one single word about his principles or his creed. . . . Let him say nothing, promise nothing. Let no committee, no convention, no town meeting ever extract from him a single word about what he thinks now, or what he will do hereafter. Let the use of pen and ink be wholly forbidden as if he were a mad poet in Bedlam."

We cherish the memory of the famous debates in 1858 between Abraham Lincoln and Stephen A. Douglas. But those debates were not part of a presidential election. When the presidency was at stake two years later, Lincoln gave no campaign speeches on the issues darkly dividing the country. He even expressed doubt about party platforms—"the formal written platform system," as he called it. The candidate's character and record, Lincoln thought, should constitute his platform: "On just such platforms all our earlier and better Presidents were elected."

However, Douglas, Lincoln's leading opponent in 1860, foreshadowed the future when he broke the sound barrier and dared venture forth on thinly disguised campaign tours. Yet Douglas established no immediate precedent. Indeed, half a dozen years later Lincoln's successor, Andrew Johnson, discredited presidential stumping by his "swing around the circle" in the midterm election of 1866. "His performances in a western tour in advocacy of his own election," commented Benjamin F. Butler, who later led the fight in Congress for Johnson's impeachment, ". . . disgusted everybody." The tenth article of impeachment charged Johnson with bringing "the high office of the President of the United States into contempt, ridicule, and disgrace" by delivering "with a loud voice certain intemperate, inflammatory, and scandalous harangues . . . peculiarly indecent and unbecoming in the Chief Magistrate of the United States."

Though presidential candidates Horatio Seymour in 1868, Rutherford B. Hayes in 1876, and James A. Garfield in 1880 made occasional speeches, only Horace Greeley in 1872, James G. Blaine in 1884, and most spectacularly, William Jennings Bryan in 1896 followed Douglas's audacious example of stumping the country. Such tactics continued to provoke disapproval. Bryan, said John Hay, who had been Lincoln's private secretary and was soon to become McKinley's secretary of state, "is begging for the presidency as a tramp might beg for a pie."

Respectable opinion still preferred the "front porch" campaign, employed by Garfield, by Benjamin Harrison in 1888, and most notably by McKinley in 1896. Here candidates received and addressed numerous delegations at their own homes—a form, as the historian Gil Troy writes, of "stumping in place."

While candidates generally continued to stand on their dignity, popular campaigning in presidential elections flourished in these years, attaining new heights of participation (82 percent of eligible voters in 1876 and never once from 1860 to 1900 under 70 percent) and new wonders of pyrotechnics and ballyhoo. Parties mobilized the electorate as never before, and political iconography was never more ingenious and fantastic. "Politics, considered not as the science of government, but as the art of winning elections and securing office," wrote the keen British observer James Bryce, "has reached in the United States a development surpassing in elaborateness that of England or France as much as the methods of those countries surpass the methods of

Servia or Roumania." Bryce marveled at the "military discipline" of the parties, at "the demonstrations, the parades and receptions, the badges and brass bands and triumphal arches," at the excitement stirred by elections—and at "the disproportion that strikes a European between the merits of the presidential candidate and the blazing enthusiasm which he evokes."

Still the old taboo held back the presidential candidates themselves. Even so irrepressible a campaigner as President Theodore Roosevelt felt obliged to hold his tongue when he ran for reelection in 1904. This unwonted abstinence reminded him, he wrote in considerable frustration, of the July day in 1898 when he was "lying still under shell fire" during the Spanish-American War. "I have continually wished that I could be on the stump myself."

No such constraint inhibited TR, however, when he ran again for the presidency in 1912. Meanwhile, and for the first time, *both* candidates in 1908—Bryan again, and William Howard Taft—actively campaigned for the prize. The duties of the office, on top of the new requirements of campaigning, led Woodrow Wilson to reflect that same year, four years before he himself ran for President, "Men of ordinary physique and discretion cannot be Presidents and live, if the strain be not somehow relieved. We shall be obliged always to be picking our chief magistrates from among wise and prudent athletes,—a small class."

Theodore Roosevelt and Woodrow Wilson combined to legitimate a new conception of presidential candidates as active molders of public opinion in active pursuit of the highest office. Once in the White House, Wilson revived the custom, abandoned by Jefferson, of delivering annual state of the union addresses to Congress in person. In 1916 he became the first incumbent President to stump for his own reelection.

The activist candidate and the bully-pulpit presidency were expressions of the growing democratization of politics. New forms of communication were reconfiguring presidential campaigns. In the nineteenth century the press, far more fiercely partisan then than today, had been the main carrier of political information. In the twentieth century the spread of advertising techniques and the rise of the electronic media—radio, television, computerized public opinion polling—wrought drastic changes in the methodology of politics. In particular the electronic age diminished and now threatens to dissolve the historic role of the party.

The old system had three tiers: the politician at one end; the voter at the other; and the party in between. The party's function was to negotiate between the politician and the voters, interpreting each to the other and providing the link that held the political process together. The electric revolution has substantially abolished the sovereignty of the party. Where once the voter turned to the local party leader to find out whom to support, now he looks at television and makes up his own mind. Where once the politician turned to the local party leader to find out what people are thinking, he now takes a computerized poll.

The electronic era has created a new breed of professional consultants, "handlers," who by the 1980s had taken control of campaigns away from the politicians. The traditional pageantry—rallies, torchlight processions, volunteers, leaflets, billboards, bumper stickers—is now largely a thing of the past. Television replaces the party as the means of mobilizing the voter. And as the party is left to wither on the vine, the presidential candidate becomes more pivotal than ever. We shall see the rise of personalist movements, founded not on historic organizations but on compelling personalities, private fortunes, and popular frustrations. Without the stabilizing influence of parties, American politics would grow angrier, wilder, and more irresponsible.

Things have changed considerably from the austerities of the old republic. Where once voters preferred to call presumably reluctant candidates to the duties of the supreme magistracy and rejected pursuit of the office as evidence of dangerous ambition, now they expect candidates to come to them, explain their views and plead for their support. Where nonpartisan virtue had been the essence, now candidates must prove to voters that they have the requisite "fire in the belly." "'Twud be inth'restin," said Mr. Dooley, ". . . if th' fathers iv th' counthry cud come back an' see what has happened while they've been away. In times past whin ye voted f'r prisident ye didn't vote f'r a man. Ye voted f'r a kind iv a statue that ye'd put up in ye'er own mind on a marble pidistal. Ye nivir heerd iv George Wash'nton goin' around th' counthry distributin' five cint see-gars."

We have reversed the original notion that ambition must be disguised and the office seek the man. Now the man—and soon, one must hope, the woman— seeks the office and does so without guilt or shame or inhibition. This is not necessarily a degradation of democracy. Dropping the disguise is a gain for candor, and personal avowals of convictions and policies may elevate and educate the electorate.

On the other hand, the electronic era has dismally reduced both the intellectual content of campaigns and the attention span of audiences. In the nineteenth century political speeches lasted for a couple of hours and dealt with issues in systematic and exhaustive fashion. Voters drove wagons for miles to hear Webster and Clay, Bryan and Teddy Roosevelt, and felt cheated if the famous orator did not give them their money's worth. Then radio came along and cut political addresses down first to an hour, soon to thirty minutes—still enough time to develop substantive arguments.

But television has shrunk the political talk first to fifteen minutes, now to the sound bite and the thirty-second spot. Advertising agencies today sell candidates with all the cynical contrivance they previously devoted to selling detergents and mouthwash. The result is the debasement of American politics. "The idea that you can merchandise candidates for high office like breakfast cereal," Adlai Stevenson said in 1952, "is the ultimate indignity to the democratic process."

Still Bryce's "intermittent fever" will be upon us every fourth year. We will continue to watch wise if not always prudent athletes in their sprint for the White House, enjoy the quadrennial spectacle and agonize about the outcome.

"The strife of the election," said Lincoln after his reelection in 1864, "is but human-nature practically applied to the facts. What has occurred in this case, must ever recur in similar cases. Human-nature will not change."

Lincoln, as usual, was right. Despite the transformation in political methods there remains a basic continuity in political emotions. "For a long while before the appointed time has come," Tocqueville wrote more than a century and a half ago, "the election becomes the important and, so to speak, the all-engrossing topic of discussion. Factional ardor is redoubled, and all the artificial passions which the imagination can create in a happy and peaceful land are agitated and brought to light. . . .

"As the election draws near, the activity of intrigue and the agitation of the populace increase; the citizens are divided into hostile camps, each of which assumes the name of its favorite candidate; the whole nation glows with feverish excitement; the election is the daily theme of the press, the subject of every private conversation, the end of every thought and every action, the sole interest of the present.

"It is true," Tocqueville added, "that as soon as the choice is determined, this ardor is dispelled, calm returns, and the river, which had nearly broken its banks, sinks to its usual level; but who can refrain from astonishment that such a storm should have arisen?"

The election storm in the end blows fresh and clean. With the tragic exception of 1860, the American people have invariably accepted the result and given the victor their hopes and blessings. For all its flaws and follies, democracy abides.

Let us now turn the pages and watch the gaudy parade of American presidential politics pass by in all its careless glory.

The Election of 2000

J. F. Watts is professor of history at The City College of New York, where he is also Dean of Humanities and the Arts. Professor Watts is the author and editor of numerous studies on American social and political history, most recently *Presidential Documents* (2000).

For more than 200 years, Election Day has marked the end of political campaigning. Election Day 2000, however, marked the beginning of a fascinating struggle between the campaigns of Vice President Al Gore and Texas governor George W. Bush. For 36 days the battle gripped national attention, the outcome swaying, in dramatic rhythm, one way then the other. Through it all, the citizenry remained calm, even developing something of a studious interest in the exotic civics lesson that played out in the struggle for that priceless reward of American political life, the White House.

Bush, who in 1994 had been elected governor of Texas in a stunning upset over incumbent Democrat Ann Richards, was a candidate for national office through pedigree, as the son of former president George Bush, as well as by electoral success. In the Texas Statehouse, he concentrated on a limited number of issues. Faced with a weak gubernatorial system that invests authority in the legislature, Bush gained stature through his charm and willingness to compromise with the agenda of the entrenched bipartisan coalition that permanently runs the Lone Star State.

By the time Bush formally announced his candidacy for the presidency in June 1999, many alternative Republican candidates still filled the political stage. Lamar Alexander, former governor of Tennessee and secretary of education under President George H. W. Bush, had good name recognition from earlier runs, sufficient financial backing, and organizational support in early primary states, particularly Iowa. Next in line came multimillionaire Steve Forbes, an indefatigable campaigner who by 1998 had moved himself distinctly to the right wing of the party. Press accounts usually mentioned former vice president Dan Quayle, and such other supplicants of the religious right as Gary Bauer, a well-known religious conservative, Senators John Ashcroft of

Missouri and Bob Smith of New Hampshire, as well as Alan Keyes, a flamboyant African-American conservative. Others included Congressman John Kasich (Ohio), Elizabeth Dole, and Governors John Engler (Michigan), Tommy Thompson (Wisconsin), and Pete Wilson (California). Most of them refused to leave without a fight. By the end of the summer of 1999, however, Governor Bush, despite his light resume and scant national standing, commanded the Republican battle for the White House. Although the GOP field remained large, the nomination was his to lose.

In October Elizabeth Dole, who was running second to Bush in GOP polls, left the race. At the same time, Arizona senator John McCain

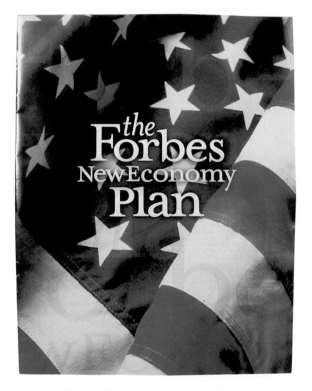

Items for Republican primary challengers appear on these pages, including buttons for Elizabeth Dole and Alan Keyes, and brochures for Steve Forbes, Dan Quayle, Keyes, and John Kasich.

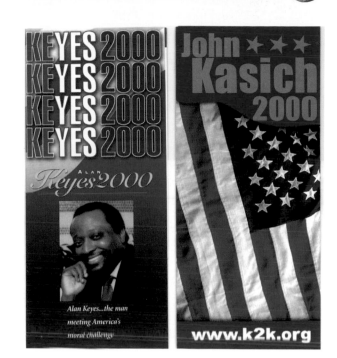

Vice President Dan Quayle
Standing Firm
for our values
★★★ Quayle 2000

Early in 1998, syndicated conservative columnist Robert Novak cited a "secret 2000 presidential 'straw poll' of Republican state chairmen" that showed overwhelming support for Governor Bush "with nobody else a close second." Republican media pundit Mary Matalin, a veteran of the 1988 and 1992 campaigns of the elder Bush, told the *Houston Chronicle* simply, "He's going to be the nominee.... He's going to be the next President of the United States."

announced his candidacy. Most observers downplayed the significance of McCain's arrival, as the senator was unpopular with the GOP establishment because of unsparing opposition to unrestricted political soft money. On February 1, 2000, however, McCain shocked Bush by defeating him by 18 points in the New Hampshire primary. Though McCain's unlikely triumph grabbed newspaper headlines and excited political pundits, the candidate who opposed soft money badly needed more of it himself. With more than $69 million in his war chest, Bush overwhelmed McCain in the primaries that followed, knocking him out of the race by mid-March.

On the Democratic side, Bush's likely opponent had also outdistanced his competition. The political force represented by Vice President Albert Gore Jr. seemed to make the campaign and the election routine precursors to the inauguration of President Gore. Gore's political presence benefited

A selection of items from the campaign of Senator John McCain.

During the early months of 2000, Senator McCain terrified powerful Republican Party interests. McCain became an authentic American hero, almost despite himself. With a record rife with rascality sufficient to sink a normal presidential candidate, the silver-haired McCain delighted in acknowledging his transgressions. As an aura of authenticity descended, the senator threatened the Bush machine in the New

Hampshire and South Carolina primaries. The measure of the man drew heavily on a daunting family legacy. Both his father and grandfather, indifferent students at Annapolis, became four-star admirals, his father rising to command all U. S. naval forces in the Pacific during the Vietnam War. Next in line, the senator, John Sidney McCain III, followed the academic legacy, graduating fifth from the bottom of his Naval Academy class.

Paid for by McCain 2000, Inc.

VOTE

JOHN McCAIN

Tuesday, Feb. 29ᵗʰ
In Virginia's Open Primary

CHARACTER, INTEGRITY, COURAGE

The High Road to the White House

NOT PAID FOR AT CAMPAIGN EXPENSE

"You will always hear the truth from me, no matter what."
John McCain

California Supports
John McCain for President

Because It's Time to Restore Honor to the Presidency

Vote McCain

MCCAIN2000.COM

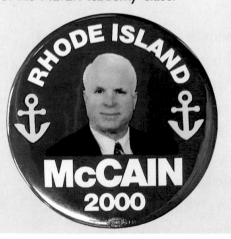

BILL BRADLEY FOR PRESIDENT. IT CAN HAPPEN.

Bill Bradley was a U.S. senator from New Jersey for 18 years. Elected without having held a lesser office in 1978, he served three full terms and chose not to seek a fourth term. Bradley's hold on political imagination rested on his apparent mastery of the basic elements of American heroism. Self-effacing, stoic, and intensely private, he appeared solemn even in the midst of the chaotic life he chose in professional basketball and politics. Handsome, athletic and intellectual, the young man from the Mississippi River town of Crystal City, Missouri, often heard elders proclaim that "he will someday be president." As a Princeton undergraduate in the early 1960s, he carried the Ivy League team to heights normally reserved for the collegiate basketball factories. As a New York Knick, he melded invaluable skills into a team concept nonpareil—"finding the open man" became a convention for teamwork. Playing beside men of obviously superior athletic skills, Bradley, silent and dependable, cool amidst howling crowds and flying elbows, prevailed. Sportswriters agreed that he "couldn't run, couldn't jump," though his career led to induction in the National Basketball League Hall of Fame.

from a portfolio of responsibilities that exceeded any of his vice-presidential predecessors. His initial deal with President Clinton included effective control of all aspects relating to the environment, but also policy formula-

American presidential election campaigns are unique among democratic nations because of their marathon character, including periods of torpor. Over nearly five months between Super Tuesday in March and the national conventions in August, Vice President Gore and Governor Bush regularly, but unsuccessfully, attempted to command public attention. The national committees of the two parties churned out press releases without discernible effect. Prominent political figures appeared on the Sunday morning talk shows, one appearance melding inconclusively into the next. "People just don't pay attention," confessed Rep. Patrick Kennedy (D-RI), head of the Democratic House campaign effort.

George W. **BUSH**

Post Office Box 1902, Austin, Texas 78767 • Phone 512/637-2000 • www.GeorgeWBush.com

GEORGE **W.** BUSH

IS FOR WOMEN

tion associated with the burgeoning Internet, bureaucratic efficiency through "reinventing government," and space and disarmament issues.

By the middle of 1999, as Bush seemed to overwhelm his Republican competitors with campaign funds, Gore jousted with the formidable former New Jersey senator Bill Bradley. This configuration defied political punditry. Gore, seven years the vice president in an administration presiding over an unprecedented bull market, should have benefited richly from peace and prosperity. Instead, going into the primary season, Bradley had raised enough money to stay in the game and even led polls in New York and California, significant Democratic redoubts. However,

Gore humbled Bradley in the Democratic primaries, and by early March the vice president's nomination was assured.

A basic rule of American politics grants presidential candidates a "bounce" in poll numbers immediately after their respective conventions, and so it was in August 2000. Governor Bush left the Republican convention in Philadelphia with a 49 to 38 percent bulge, but Vice President Gore came to prevail after the Democratic convention in Los Angeles by 52 to 48 percent. In fact, the early stages of the fall campaign made clear the nearly even split between the men that would prevail until the bitter end.

Neither Gore nor Bush possessed the natural political magic on the campaign trail of a Reagan or Clinton. Both thus spent the several weeks prior to the first debate in early October perfecting modes of attack, defense, and image projection. One or both candidates would eventually appear with Regis Philbin, Rosie O'Donnell, and Jay Leno, and on *Saturday Night Live*, whose caustic satires portrayed Bush as stupid and Gore as robotic. That even Green Party presidential candidate Ralph Nader, a notoriously unfunny man, appeared on Letterman

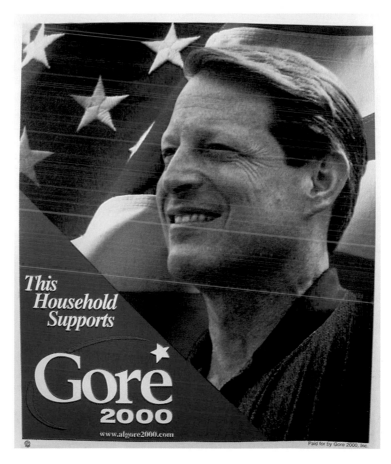

This Household Supports

Gore 2000

www.algore2000.com

Paid for by Gore 2000, Inc.

Items from the third-party campaigns, including a Pat Buchanan (Reform Party) brochure, and buttons for Ralph Nader (Green Party) and the Reform ticket of Buchanan and Ezola Foster. Neither party presented a serious challenge: Nader received about 2.7 percent of the vote, Buchanan less than 0.5 percent. Nevertheless, Nader's name on the Florida presidential ballot probably cost Gore the election.

best proves the point of permanently altered campaign requirements.

The major contenders went into their first debate on October 3 dead-locked at about 45 percent each. Nader stood at 4 percent, while Pat Buchanan, the candidate of the Reform Party, hovered at an unsteady 1 percent. The Commission on Presidential Debates excluded candidates who failed to achieve at least a 15 percent rating in several polls, thus denying Buchanan and Nader a chance to participate in the scheduled debates. Both protested mightily, Nader actually being carted away by police and threatened with arrest. Buchanan never became a factor in the race; Nader persisted, significantly so.

During the first debate, Gore warned that Bush tax cuts would endanger the integrity of Medicare and Social Security. Facts came as drumbeats sounding across the territory of foreign and domestic accomplishments and prospects. Bush popped in with vague general responses, emphasizing

The first presidential debate between Gore and Bush was held on October 3, 2000. The two were deadlocked in the Gallup Poll with about 45 percent each. The Commission on Presidential Debates held to a ruling excluding candidates who failed to achieve at least 15 percent in several polls, thus denying Pat Buchanan (about 1 percent) and Ralph Nader (4 percent) participation. Both protested mightily; when Nader showed up at the hall where the debate was held, he was escorted out by police and threatened with arrest.

A Gallup Poll conducted immediately after the first debate revealed that among registered voters who watched the two candidates exchange views on a variety of issues, 48 percent thought Gore had done the better job, while 41 percent believed Bush had. When asked to rate each candidate individually on how well he'd performed in the debate, 76 percent said Gore had done an excellent or good job, compared with 70 percent for Bush. However, these results reflected voters' immediate reactions, before they had an opportunity to discuss the debates with friends and colleagues and to be exposed to the media coverage of the event.

that he supported individuals while Gore favored government. While Bush spoke, Gore's facial gestures suggested disgust, which he underscored with audible heavy sighs.

In the second debate, the candidates interacted only with PBS anchor Jim Lehrer in what was billed as "a more informal exchange." The three men sat around a table and proceeded through the familiar litany of domestic and international items. Analysts noted two principal differences in this second contest. Bush, well briefed and sharp on foreign policy matters, seemed confident and "presidential." Gore, reacting to earlier criticism, softened his posture markedly. Tracking polls continued to predict a dead heat.

A few days later, the last debate unfolded in a "town hall" format thought to favor the more experienced Gore. Both men were able to move around the stage, back and forth toward the audience and toward each other, while exchanging barbs. Gore seemed much more aggressive in affirming and parrying points on health care, size of government, and taxes. Bush held his own, at one dramatic point effectively muting an

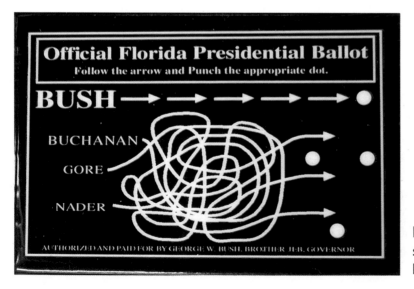

Post-election button satirizing the Florida butterfly ballot.

accusatory question from the audience on capital punishment in Texas. The polls reflected a tie as Election Day arrived.

To win the presidency, Gore or Bush needed 270 electoral votes. As the returns were tallied on election night, the national television news outlets predicted Gore the winner, then announced that Bush had in fact won, and finally declared that no one had yet won the election, as the vote in Florida was "too close to call." Gore had 266 electoral votes, Bush 246; Florida's 25 electoral votes would determine the 43rd president of the United States.

Bush had apparently won the state by a few hundred votes, but Florida law requires a recount when the difference between contenders is less than 0.005 percent. Election officials across the state immediately began to recount nearly 6 million votes, and await overseas ballots. The Republican secretary of state, Katherine Harris, would certify the results. Governor Jeb Bush recused himself from official participation in his brother's struggle.

"Recount," of course, immediately became a misnomer. Cries of deception and intimidation had arisen in South Florida even before the polls closed, first with the suddenly infamous "butterfly ballot." These were poorly designed manual ballots that opponents contended made it easy to vote for the wrong candidate. In one Palm Beach County district, 3,407 "butterfly ballot" votes for Pat Buchanan constituted about 20 percent of his entire total statewide. A later survey failed to find one voter who favored Buchanan. As the days passed, powerful teams representing both candidates arrived in Florida to haggle. Within the next few hours, tens of thousands of "butterfly ballots" would be deemed invalid, punched twice, arguably out of frustration after a "mistake."

Lawyers, public relations staffers, and political operatives skilled in the covert machinations common to political crises loomed up around the state. Former secretary of state Warren Christopher, a veteran of emergencies foreign and domestic, headed the Gore forces. Former secretary of state James A. Baker III, a Bush family loyalist thought to have absorbed some blame for President Bush's failure in 1992, marshaled the team of George Bush the younger.

Immediately, both sides went to court. Thus began an often-obscure war of injunctions, stays, and appeals that would rage for a month and stop only at the United States Supreme Court. On Saturday, November 11, Bush's forces went into Federal District Court in Miami to protest the

Ceramic coffee mug. As Election Day 2000 passed westward from the Atlantic coast toward remote Alaska and distant Hawaii, early returns, exit polls, and trend analysis continued. Despite the well-cultivated illusion that one or another group of familiar faces possessed special insight, all information came from the same source, produced by Voter News Service, a consortium created for the occasion by ABC, CBS, NBC, Fox, and the Associated Press.

"arbitrary and unconstrained decision-making authority" ostensibly practiced by local election officials presiding over recounts. Shortly thereafter, as if to focus the issue, officials in heavily Democratic Palm Beach County ordered the review of 425,000 votes, including those where the "chad" had not fully cleared the hole in the ballot. Page one of the *New York Times* on Sunday, November 12, featured a photograph of a Florida judge holding a "dangling chad" up to the light, flanked by a Republican observer on one shoulder and a Democrat on the other.

The Miami federal judge rejected the Republican bid to halt recounts. As they continued, Harris, a member of Governor Jeb Bush's cabinet, told reporters that within hours she would enforce a deadline for the reporting of all official vote tallies from across the state. The Democrats prevailed against Harris in state court. The recounting continued, Bush's lead bobbing slightly at just a few hundred votes. The political warfare escalated.

On November 15, a Wednesday evening, Gore unexpectedly went on national television. In deliberate and mannerly fashion, he spoke of the reasonableness of supplementing voting machine counts ("Machines can sometimes misread or fail to detect the way ballots are cast") with "complete hand counts," specifically in Palm Beach County, Miami-Dade County, and Broward County. If Bush wished, he continued, the entire state could be recounted. Whatever the method chosen, Gore stressed, "I will abide by the result, I will take no legal action to challenge the result, and I will not support any legal action to challenge the result." Gore concluded by calling for a personal meeting with Bush "to reaffirm our national unity."

The Republican forces responded with a two-pronged counterattack. Shortly after Gore's television appearance, Katherine Harris announced that it was her "duty under Florida law" to reject any county's request to update totals. Meanwhile, the Bush forces, shocked by Gore's unexpected prime time broadcast, sprung into action. Bush hurriedly left his ranch and raced 100 miles to the governor's mansion in Austin. Just over three hours after Gore's appearance, and reflecting the emergency nature of the situation, Bush effectively responded. He opposed recounts because the standards varied from county to county, appearing subjective and arbitrary. The votes had already been counted and recounted, he argued, and "the way to conclude this election in a fair and accurate and final way is for the State of Florida to count the remaining overseas ballots, add them to the certified vote and announce the results, as required by Florida law." There would be no meeting between the two men.

As the ides of November passed, the nation remained manifestly calm, yet the nonstop political talk shows inherited dramatic new material every day. The Florida Supreme Court made its first appearance on the national stage with a ruling that Palm Beach and Broward Counties, putatively Democratic, could continue recounts. Gore forces also went to court to stop Secretary Harris from refusing to accept fresh tallies. Bush lawyers traveled to Atlanta with an appeal to the United States Court of Appeals for

Rectangular button for Gore and Hillary Clinton, who was running for New York's U.S. Senate seat previously held by Daniel Patrick Moynihan. Clinton trounced Republican Rick Lazio to become the first First Lady elected to a political position.

Throughout the campaign, the Gore political strategists held the strong belief that close association with either Bill or Hillary Clinton represented a political liability. This decision might have cost Gore the electoral votes of either Arkansas or Tennessee—and the election.

Humorous celluloid button supporting President Josiah Bartlett, played by Martin Sheen on a popular television show about the White House, *The West Wing*.

the Eleventh Circuit, arguing that the absence of clear state criteria for counting votes amounted to an unconstitutional violation of voting rights. The Bush lead held at 300 votes.

Back in Tallahassee, the Florida Supreme Court ruled that the state could not certify the result. First, the court had to rule on the disputed votes still being examined in the three heavily Democratic counties, as well as add in the overseas tallies that continued to arrive.

Ten days after Election Day, Bush's lead in the Florida popular vote stood at 750. Beside that modest number towered the figure of 1.5 million votes to be recounted in areas with a strong Gore predisposition. A further blow to Bush came from Atlanta, where the Circuit Court refused to halt recounts. Some decidedly good news for Bush accompanied the completion of overseas ballots: his lead inched upward to 930.

The spotlight shifted to the seven justices of the Florida Supreme Court, six of them more or less identified with the Democrats. During oral arguments, Chief Justice Charles T. Wells discussed the significance of the date December 12 with Gore attorney David Boies. He asked Boies if all aspects of Florida voting "have to be finally determined by that date. . . . Do you agree with that?" Boies admitted that he did. The date in question, sometimes referred to as a "safe harbor," would allow for the designation of Florida electors in time for the December 18 meeting of the electoral college. Boies's admission would later be used against him in the strongest measure.

On November 22, the court unanimously held that the South Florida recounts should proceed to completion within the following five days. The justices provided no definitive formula for evaluating the variety of chads.

In Miami, the largest reservoir of potential votes for Gore simply disappeared. Miami-Dade County, the largest enclave of Democratic votes in the state, abruptly decided not to continue with recounts. The official reason cited an inability to meet the deadline four days hence. This immediately followed a threatening series of events at the office of the election supervisor, where protesters advanced into the building to the room where the canvassing board sat, banged on the door, and shouted "voter fraud" and "let us in." Sheriff's deputies arrived to protect a surrounded local Democratic official. Two cameramen went to the ground in the melee. Shortly thereafter, the board abandoned the recount.

As the Gore forces recoiled, wire services announced that Bush had requested the intervention of the United States Supreme Court. The language addressed to the Court reflected the increasing panic of the situation. The recount process was "selective, capricious and standardless . . . riddled with severe and pervasive irregularities . . . manifest inconsistencies in counting methods and a politically charged, partisan atmosphere, all of which have combined to spawn a process that now borders on anarchy." To general amazement, the Supreme Court ordered arguments on *Bush v. Gore*.

Regardless, within 48 hours of the Supreme Court bombshell, Florida's secretary of state Katherine Harris announced Bush's "official" capture of the Florida popular vote, his margin put at 537, and thus Florida's 25 electoral votes. That would produce one more than the 270 minimum needed for victory. Bush went before cameras in Austin and claimed the presidency. Gore refused to concede, and announced another round of court proceedings. In fact, all over Florida, more than 100 attorneys pursued lawsuits on both sides. Bush forces had suits against several counties over

Ceramic coffee mugs: Gore-Lieberman and Bush-Cheney.

the question of counting overseas ballots. "Private citizens" sued Seminole County over thousands of absentee ballots. Two "citizens' suits" contested the legality of the "butterfly ballot." In Washington, the Supreme Court had taken under advisement *Bush v. Gore.*

Meanwhile, the state legislature added to the political tension. The Republican-dominated legislature, also with an eye on time, declared its interest in a special session for the purpose of designating the state's 25 electors, who would be pledged to Bush. A constitutional nightmare loomed. Should Gore prevail in the courts, and in ensuing recounts, eventually winning the state, a slate of electors would emerge pledged to him. Two slates of electors? Only in the corrupted 1876 election had the political system frozen so solid.

All the legal warfare would soon be mooted merely by the passage of time. The inevitable turn of the calendar posed the greatest danger for Gore. Florida's electors would have to be designated before the "safe harbor"

Nader rally notice.

Ralph Nader, consumer advocate and leader of the consumer protection movement, graduated from Princeton University in 1955 and received a law degree from Harvard in 1958. Nader and his associates did not invent consumer advocacy. However, they did transform its meaning, focusing on fact-finding research and government lobbying for new laws on key consumer issues. In 1996, when he first ran for president, he received about 700,000 votes, less than 1 percent. In 2000, as the Green Party's nominee, he managed to secure about 3 percent of the total vote—falling short of the 5 percent minimum necessary to receive federal election funds in future presidential campaigns.

of December 12, a date six days prior to the meeting of the electoral college itself. Gore's case before Leon County circuit judge N. Saunders Sauls began in Tallahassee on December 3. The judge had refused to permit ongoing recounts before or during the case, although he did allow disputed ballots to be transported from South Florida to the capital city in the north.

With a national television audience watching, Judge Sauls listened carefully to minute descriptions of chad varieties and their putative legitimacy, or lack thereof. Regarding the disputed ballots, Boies, a celebrated New York litigator and head of the Gore law assemblage, maintained, "There is sufficient evidence that those votes could change or at least place in doubt the results of the election." His counterpart, Barry Richard, perhaps the most powerful local presence in any Florida courtroom, retorted that such consideration required

> that this court should disregard all of the actions of the various canvassing boards that are under challenge here and should begin anew an assessment and a count of all of the votes that the plaintiffs challenge.

Thus began the nine-hour Saturday session. Convoluted questions and extended answers, objections, and responses dragged out the hours, to the consternation of the Gore camp. The Sunday session would be even worse for them. At the end of the 14-hour day, Sauls provided a grace note for both sides, saying, "I suppose at this time, counsel, I must tell you it was a case well tried and argued." Outside both Boies and Richard proclaimed their optimism. Judgment came swiftly.

The very next day, December 4, Judge Sauls rejected every argument advanced by Gore's lawyers. They failed, he said, to prove a "reasonable probability" that the election results would be different had disputed ballots been counted. Sauls told a hushed courtroom that "the evidence does not establish any illegality, dishonesty, gross negligence, improper influence, coercion or fraud in the balloting and counting processes." One Bush lawyer exulted, "This was as complete a victory as I've ever gotten in a trial."

On Friday and Saturday, December 8 and 9, as never before, the American political system disappeared into courthouses. On Friday, an angry and divided Florida Supreme Court, voting 4 to 3, ordered a recount "in all Florida counties where there was an undervote"—that is, a review of approximately 45,000 cases where a ballot recorded no vote for president. Canvassing officials were to begin the next day, Saturday, and conclude by 2 P.M. on Sunday. The majority opinion took the approach that Judge Sauls had erred by misinterpreting the law at several key points. It alluded to widely aired complaints of irregularities from African-American districts in Miami-Dade County, concluding that "although the time constraints are limited, we must do everything required by law to ensure that legal votes that have not been counted are included in the final election results." Governor Bush's legal team immediately appealed the ruling to the U.S. Supreme Court.

The next day, as the recounting continued, a veritable scoreboard reflected the tally. Bush led by 154 votes (or 191). At 2:45 P.M. ET, as a significant national audience watched officials in several Florida districts try to "recount the undercount," a bulletin staggered the country. From Washington, suddenly and against all odds, the Supreme Court of the United States, split 5 to 4, ordered the immediate halt of all electoral board activities in Florida. The Court's majority consisted of Chief Justice William H. Rehnquist and Justices Sandra Day O'Connor, Antonin Scalia, Anthony M. Kennedy, and Clarence Thomas. Dissenting were Justices John Paul Stevens, David H. Souter, Ruth Bader Ginsburg, and Steven G. Breyer. The deep and complex divide among the nine men and women could not have been more fundamental.

On the simple question of appropriate jurisdiction, "liberals" and "conservatives" had reversed positions. The conservative majority faced the paradox of overruling the authority of a state supreme court, a familiar fault line in the American federal system in which the conservative legacy had resolutely opposed centralization of power. The Court's "liberals" would support the authority and decision of the state court, reversing the tradition of such jurists to champion federal judicial supremacy. More immediately, accepting and deciding *Bush v. Gore* would mock the Court's historic attempt to preserve its majesty through insulation from party politics.

On Monday morning, December 11, the justices assembled to hear once more the now-familiar arguments. From the Bush side, led by Theodore B. Olsen, longtime Republican legal luminary in Washington, the theme would be that recounting in Florida was both illegal and unconstitutional. The Gore forces, again directed by David Boies, would maintain "the right of voters to have their ballots counted." For 90 minutes, the most intense legal seminar in American history took place before a select audience, with millions following a near-simultaneous audio transcription.

The justices set the tone immediately. A minute or so after launching into his opening, Olsen heard Justice Kennedy demand, "Can you begin by telling us our federal jurisdiction? Where's the federal question here?" Olsen responded, and the colloquies soon involved all other justices except Clarence Thomas, who, in his usual fashion, remained mute. Souter and Breyer angled for a position that would establish a single criterion for recounting, with an eye to sending the case back to Florida. Scalia, on the opposite approach, inquired regarding chads and stated the view that imperfect perforations were the result of mistakes made by voters, a situation that did not produce a wrong. Rehnquist sought clarification on some facts. O'Connor probed the murky area between legislative and judicial authority; Stevens picked up O'Connor's point, questioning Olsen's contention that the Florida Supreme Court did not possess sufficient authority to review the legislature's electoral design. Ginsburg further developed the Souter-Breyer theme of finding a universally acceptable standard for recounting.

The Gore team's strategy depended on attracting as swing votes O'Connor and Kennedy. To that end, Boies advanced the

Celluloid Bush-Cheney button. The National Rifle Association (NRA) endorsed Bush.

proposition of the appropriateness of the Florida court's 4-3 ruling ordering the resumption of recounts. Here the case hung for the continuation of Gore hopes. Neither swing vote appeared to move, both justices taking Boies to task on the implications of his argument. "We can't send this back for more fact-finding," a laconic Souter admitted.

Office lights in the Court building burned through the night on Monday. The next day a large part of the nation hovered near television sets. Public opinion remained remarkably calm even as commentators pointed to an eventual loss of patience, with all that implied. On the Court grounds the media remained poised. Just after 10 P.M. ET, the undercurrent rose. "Something is happening," television viewers were told. A bizarre tableau immediately materialized.

Television "runners" were seen grabbing at the sheaves of paper coming from the Court's press office. They ran, literally, to the waiting reporters, who tried to make sense of what they held in their hands, turning pages, scanning, producing instant interpretation, all the while live on the networks and cable channels.

As viewers flipped channels over the next hour, they received wildly different accounts of the meaning of the 67-page decision. Several journalists

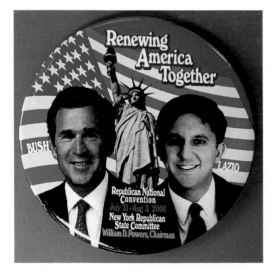

and their legal pundits believed the court would allow the Florida recounts to proceed. Dan Rather of CBS thought that the opinion did not make Bush president. Pete Williams and Dan Abrams of MSNBC surmised the opposite. CNN's Bernard Shaw, Judy Woodruff, and Roger Cossack clung to the determination that Florida would recount.

Clarity formed overnight. For the first time in American history, the United

(Right) Bush post-card featuring the president-elect and his wife, Laura. (Opposite) Button for Bush and Rick Lazio, a four-term congressman from New York running for the state's open U.S. Senate seat. Lazio lost the election to Hillary Rodham Clinton.

States Supreme Court effectively chose the president of the United States. The Court divided 5 to 4, the same majority that had accepted jurisdiction in *Bush v. Gore*. The majority opinion stressed the approach of midnight, the "safe harbor" date of December 12. Time had run out, the justices held, making it impossible to recount votes while at the same time respecting "minimal constitutional standards." Boies's earlier admission of the "safe harbor" deadline had returned to haunt him.

Justices Souter, Breyer, and Ginsburg had agreed that the lack of a standard threatened equal protection. With vehemence, however, the dissenters argued the necessity of creating that standard and proceeding with the recount. They lost.

In the media, most legal commentators were hostile to the decision. Some suggested the decision might establish troubling precedents in fed-eral-state judicial relations or in the interpretation of equal protection. All of the justices in the majority had lengthy records in opposition to an elastic (or "liberal") interpretation of the equal protection clause, until they embraced it in *Bush v. Gore*. Conservative scholars, supporting the decision, stressed the necessity of averting a burgeoning national crisis if

George Bush succeeded Bill Clinton, who left office with the highest average job approval rating of any president in the previous 50 years, but with low public ratings of his personal character—a conflicted view of Clinton that emerged during the Monica Lewinsky scandal and ensuing impeachment trial.

According to a Gallup Poll conducted January 5–7, 2001, 65 percent of Americans approved of the way Clinton handled his job as president, which was slightly above the average he had received between October and December 2000. In fact, Clinton's average approval rating for his last two years in office was about 61 percent—the highest rating for a final quarter of a presidential tenure in the last half century. On the other hand, in the same survey, just 41 percent of Americans approved of Clinton "as a person" and only 39 percent considered him "honest and trustworthy." By a substantial margin, 68 percent to 28 percent, Americans expected Clinton to be remembered more for his involvement in personal scandal than for his accomplishments. And, on the last day of his presidency, Clinton admitted to what most Americans had long concluded: that he had testified falsely in the sexual harassment lawsuit that had lit the fuse to the impeachment bombshell, unleashing anguish and bitter political combat.

the public rose in frustration, or, more likely, if a bitterly partisan Congress staged a reenactment of 1876.

In the frenzied hours after the decision, Gore's strategists in Washington and Florida, encouraged by the vice president, scrutinized the majority opinion seeking mechanisms that would allow his campaign to continue. They continued through the night and into the new day before bowing to a rising consensus, even among partisan supporters, that Gore concede.

On December 13—36 days after Election Day—the president-elect of the United States addressed the nation from the chamber of the Texas

House of Representatives in the capitol building in Austin. The Speaker of the House, Democrat Pete Laney, introduced Bush to a jubilant throng. "I was elected not to serve one party, but to serve one nation," Bush insisted. "Whether you voted for me or not, I will do my best to serve your interests, and I will work to earn your respect."

An hour earlier, Al Gore had placed a brief call to concede personally to "the president-elect," the first time he had used the term, and to offer formal congratulations. Gore had then gone on national television for an eight-minute speech widely characterized as eloquent and gracious. He emphasized his disagreement with the Court's decision, but said, "I offer my concession."

The final certified tallies showed that Gore won the popular vote by about 500,000, winning 20 states and the District of Columbia, with 266 electoral votes. Bush won 30 states and 271 electoral votes, one more than the needed majority in the Electoral College. Florida's deciding tally of 537 votes, out of the officially counted 5,825,043, captured the conclusive 25 electoral votes. Who "won" Florida? "No one is ever going to know," said Illinois Republican congressman John Shimkus. "There will be a burden to acknowledge that."

On Inauguration Day, a uniquely American tragicomedy unfolded with all the characters present: presidents Bush, Clinton, and Bush; rejected former vice president Gore; Chief Justice Rehnquist, who presided over Clinton's impeachment and the younger Bush's ascension; and the eight other justices, who milled about each other now—away from the center of the stage.

GEORGE WALKER BUSH

- **Born:** July 6, 1946, in New Haven, Connecticut
- **Parents:** George and Barbara Pierce Bush
- **Education:** Graduated from Yale University in 1968, and Harvard Business School in 1975
- **Occupation:** businessman, baseball team owner, public official
- **Married:** Laura Welch (1946–   ) on November 5, 1977
- **Children:** Barbara Pierce Bush (1981–   ); Jenna Welch Bush (1981–   )

Served as the 43RD PRESIDENT OF THE UNITED STATES,

- January 20, 2001, to present

VICE PRESIDENT

- Richard Cheney (2001–   )

OTHER POLITICAL POSITIONS

- Governor of Texas, 1995–2000

CABINET

Secretary of State
• Colin Luther Powell (2001–   )

Secretary of the Treasury
• Paul O'Neill (2001–   )

Secretary of Defense
• Donald H. Rumsfeld (2001–   )

Attorney General
• John Ashcroft (2001–   )

Secretary of the Interior
• Gale Norton (2001–   )

Secretary of Agriculture
• Ann Veneman (2001–   )

Secretary of Commerce
• Don Evans (2001–   )

Secretary of Labor
• Elaine Chao (2001–   )

**Secretary of Health
and Human Services**
• Tommy G. Thompson (2001–   )

**Secretary of Housing
and Urban Development**
• Mel Martinez (2001–   )

Secretary of Transportation
• Norman Y. Mineta (2001–   )

Secretary of Energy
• Spencer Abraham (2001–   )

Secretary of Education
• Roderick R. Paige (2001–   )

Secretary of Veterans Affairs
• Anthony Principi (2001–   )

NOTABLE EVENTS DURING BUSH'S ADMINISTRATION

2001   On January 20, George W. Bush is sworn in as the 43rd president of the United States; in June, Bush signs the Economic Growth and Tax Relief Reconciliation Act, which provides a series of tax cuts that are phased in over a ten-year period; on September 11, terrorists fly hijacked airplanes into the World Trade Center in New York and the Pentagon in Washington, D.C.; on October 7, air strikes begin against Afghanistan, which is suspected of harboring Osama bin Laden, the terrorist leader who ordered the September 11 attacks; the next day, the president creates the Office of Homeland Security by executive order, naming Pennsylvania Governor Tom Ridge its director.

2002   On May 24, Bush signs treaty with Russian president Vladimir Putin to reduce levels of nuclear weapons; on June 24, calls for new Palestinian leadership to replace Yasser Arafat so that the peace process with Israel can continue; in July, presents the Strategy for Homeland Security proposal to Congress.

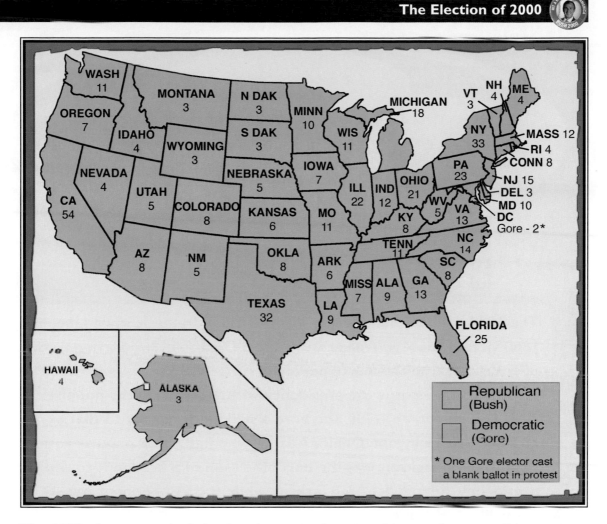

The 2000 election marked the fourth time in American history that a candidate won a majority of the popular vote, but lost the presidency in the electoral college. (The other elections were 1824, 1876, and 1888.) Al Gore received 50,996,582 votes and carried 20 states, totalling 266 electoral votes; George W. Bush won more states but about half a million fewer votes (50,456,062). However, the Supreme Court ruling that ended the disputed Florida recount meant that state's 25 electoral votes went to Bush, giving him 271 and the presidency.

Bush v. Gore Supreme Court Opinion

The 2000 presidential election was the most dramatic since Lincoln's 1860 victory. George Walker Bush, the 54-year-old, two-term governor of Texas, became the fourth person in American history, and the first since 1888, to assume the presidency without winning the popular vote. The election of 2000 also bore a striking similarity to that of 1824. In that year, John Quincy Adams, who had fewer popular votes than Andrew Jackson, was the only other son of a president to win the presidency. Adams defeated Jackson while Bush's opponent was Al Gore, like Jackson a Tennessean.

Bush won the election after a 36-day bruising legal battle over Florida's 25 electoral votes, a state in which his brother Jeb was governor. The Florida election was finally decided by the nine U.S. Supreme Court justices who bitterly split over the issues. Bush was elected with 271 electoral votes, just one more than the minimum. Future historians will analyze this fascinating election in detail. For example, it can be argued that the Constitution of the United States provides a political solution for such an election through the legislative branch—but, in our federal system of government, there also exists a judicial remedy. It is this option which decided the final outcome.

Per Curiam.

I

On December 8, 2000, the Supreme Court of Florida ordered that the Circuit Court of Leon County tabulate by hand 9,000 ballots in Miami-Dade County. It also ordered the inclusion in the certified vote totals of 215 votes identified in Palm Beach County and 168 votes identified in Miami-Dade County for Vice President Albert Gore, Jr., and Senator Joseph Lieberman, Democratic Candidates for President and Vice President. The Supreme Court noted that petitioner, Governor George W. Bush, asserted that the net gain for Vice President Gore in Palm Beach County was 176 votes, and directed the Circuit Court to resolve that dispute on remand. [. . .] The court further held that relief would require manual recounts in all Florida counties where so-called "undervotes" had not been subject to manual tabulation. The court ordered all manual recounts to begin at once. Governor Bush and Richard Cheney, Republican Candidates for the Presidency and Vice Presidency, filed an emergency application for a stay of this mandate. On December 9, we granted the application, treated the application as a petition for a writ of certiorari, and granted certiorari. *Post*, p. ___.

The proceedings leading to the present controversy are discussed in some detail in our opinion in *Bush v. Palm Beach County Canvassing Bd.*, *ante*, p. ___ (*per curiam*) (*Bush I*). On November 8, 2000, the day following the Presidential election, the Florida Division of Elections reported that petitioner, Governor Bush, had received 2,909,135 votes, and respondent, Vice President Gore, had received 2,907,351 votes, a margin of 1,784 for Governor Bush. Because Governor Bush's margin of victory was less than "one-half of a percent . . . of the votes cast," an automatic machine recount was conducted under §102.141(4) of the election code, the results of which showed Governor Bush still winning the race but by a diminished margin. Vice President Gore then sought manual recounts in Volusia, Palm Beach, Broward, and Miami-Dade Counties, pursuant to Florida's election protest provisions. Fla. Stat. §102.166 (2000). A dispute arose concerning the deadline for local county canvassing boards to submit their returns to the Secretary of State (Secretary). The Secretary declined to waive the November 14 deadline imposed by statute. §§102.111, 102.112. The Florida Supreme Court, however, set the deadline at November 26. We granted certiorari and vacated the Florida Supreme Court's decision, finding considerable uncertainty as to the grounds on which it was based. *Bush I, ante*, at ___–___ (slip. op., at 6–7). On December 11, the Florida Supreme Court issued a decision on remand reinstating that date. ___ So. 2d ___, ___ (slip op. at 30–31).

On November 26, the Florida Elections Canvassing Commission certified the results of the election and declared Governor Bush the winner of Florida's 25 electoral votes. On November 27, Vice President Gore, pursuant to Florida's contest provisions, filed a complaint in Leon County Circuit Court contesting the certification. Fla. Stat. §102.168 (2000). He sought relief pursuant to §102.168(3)(c), which provides that "[r]eceipt of a number of illegal votes or rejection of a number of legal votes sufficient to change or place in doubt the result of the election" shall be grounds for a contest. The Circuit Court denied relief, stating that Vice President Gore failed to meet his burden of proof. He appealed to the First District Court of Appeal, which certified the matter to the Florida Supreme Court.

Accepting jurisdiction, the Florida Supreme Court affirmed in part and reversed in part. *Gore v. Harris*, ___ So. 2d. ___ (2000). The court held that the Circuit Court had been correct to reject Vice President Gore's challenge to the results certified in Nassau County and his challenge to the Palm Beach County Canvassing Board's determination that 3,300 ballots cast in that county were not, in the statutory phrase, "legal votes."

The Supreme Court held that Vice President Gore had satisfied his burden of proof under §102.168(3)(c) with respect to his challenge to Miami-Dade

County's failure to tabulate, by manual count, 9,000 ballots on which the machines had failed to detect a vote for President ("undervotes"). ___ So. 2d., at ___ (slip. op., at 22–23). Noting the closeness of the election, the Court explained that "[o]n this record, there can be no question that there are legal votes within the 9,000 uncounted votes sufficient to place the results of this election in doubt." *Id*., at ___ (slip. op., at 35). A "legal vote," as determined by the Supreme Court, is "one in which there is a 'clear indication of the intent of the voter.'" *Id*., at ___ (slip op., at 25). The court therefore ordered a hand recount of the 9,000 ballots in Miami-Dade County. Observing that the contest provisions vest broad discretion in the circuit judge to "provide any relief appropriate under such circumstances," Fla. Stat. §102.168(8) (2000), the Supreme Court further held that the Circuit Court could order "the Supervisor of Elections and the Canvassing Boards, as well as the necessary public officials, in all counties that have not conducted a manual recount or tabulation of the undervotes . . . to do so forthwith, said tabulation to take place in the individual counties where the ballots are located." ___ So. 2d, at ___ (slip. op., at 38).

The Supreme Court also determined that both Palm Beach County and Miami-Dade County, in their earlier manual recounts, had identified a net gain of 215 and 168 legal votes for Vice President Gore. *Id*., at ___ (slip. op., at 33–34). Rejecting the Circuit Court's conclusion that Palm Beach County lacked the authority to include the 215 net votes submitted past the November 26 deadline, the Supreme Court explained that the deadline was not intended to exclude votes identified after that date through ongoing manual recounts. As to Miami-Dade County, the Court concluded that although the 168 votes identified were the result of a partial recount, they were "legal votes [that] could change the outcome of the election." *Id*., at (slip op., at 34). The Supreme Court therefore directed the Circuit Court to include those totals in the certified results, subject to resolution of the actual vote total from the Miami-Dade partial recount.

The petition presents the following questions: whether the Florida Supreme Court established new standards for resolving Presidential election contests, thereby violating Art. II, §1, cl. 2, of the United States Constitution and failing to comply with 3 U.S.C. § 5 and whether the use of standardless manual recounts violates the Equal Protection and Due Process Clauses. With respect to the equal protection question, we find a violation of the Equal Protection Clause.

II

A

The closeness of this election, and the multitude of legal challenges which have followed in its wake, have brought into sharp focus a common, if heretofore unnoticed, phenomenon. Nationwide statistics reveal that an estimated 2% of ballots cast do not register a vote for President for whatever reason, including deliberately choosing no candidate at all or some voter error, such as voting for two candidates or insufficiently marking a ballot. See Ho, More Than 2M Ballots Uncounted, AP Online (Nov. 28, 2000); Kelley, Balloting Problems Not Rare But Only In A Very Close Election Do Mistakes And Mismarking Make A Difference, Omaha World-Herald (Nov. 15, 2000). In certifying election results, the votes eligible for inclusion in the certification are the votes meeting the properly established legal requirements.

This case has shown that punch card balloting machines can produce an unfortunate number of ballots which are not punched in a clean, complete way by the voter. After the current counting, it is likely legislative bodies nationwide will examine ways to improve the mechanisms and machinery for voting.

B

The individual citizen has no federal constitutional right to vote for electors for the President of the United States unless and until the state legislature chooses a statewide election as the means to implement its power to appoint members of the Electoral College. U.S. Const., Art. II, §1. This is the source for the statement in *McPherson v. Blacker*, 146 U.S. 1, 35 (1892), that the State legislature's power to select the manner for appointing electors is plenary; it may, if it so chooses, select the electors itself, which indeed was the manner used by State legislatures in several States for many years after the Framing of our Constitution. *Id.*, at 28–33. History has now favored the voter, and in each of the several States the citizens themselves vote for Presidential electors. When the state legislature vests the right to vote for President in its people, the right to vote as the legislature has prescribed is fundamental; and one source of its fundamental nature lies in the equal weight accorded to each vote and the equal dignity owed to each voter. The State, of course, after granting the franchise in the special context of Article II, can take back the power to appoint electors. See *id.*, at 35 ("[T]here is no doubt of the right of the legislature to resume the power at any time, for it can neither be taken away nor abdicated") (quoting S. Rep. No. 395, 43d Cong., 1st Sess.).

The right to vote is protected in more than the initial allocation of the franchise. Equal protection applies as well to the manner of its exercise. Having once granted the right to vote on equal terms, the State may not, by later arbitrary and disparate treatment, value one person's vote over that of another. See, *e.g.*, *Harper v. Virginia Bd. of Elections*, 383 U.S. 663, 665 (1966) ("[O]nce the franchise is granted to the electorate, lines may not be drawn which are inconsistent with the Equal Protection Clause of the Fourteenth Amendment"). It must be remembered that "the right of suffrage can be denied by a debasement or dilution of the weight of a citizen's vote just as effectively as by wholly prohibiting the free exercise of the franchise." *Reynolds v. Sims*, 377 U.S. 533, 555 (1964).

There is no difference between the two sides of the present controversy on these basic propositions. Respondents say that the very purpose of vindicating the right to vote justifies the recount procedures now at issue. The question before us, however, is whether the recount procedures the Florida Supreme

Court has adopted are consistent with its obligation to avoid arbitrary and disparate treatment of the members of its electorate.

Much of the controversy seems to revolve around ballot cards designed to be perforated by a stylus but which, either through error or deliberate omission, have not been perforated with sufficient precision for a machine to count them. In some cases a piece of the card—a chad—is hanging, say by two corners. In other cases there is no separation at all, just an indentation.

The Florida Supreme Court has ordered that the intent of the voter be discerned from such ballots. For purposes of resolving the equal protection challenge, it is not necessary to decide whether the Florida Supreme Court had the authority under the legislative scheme for resolving election disputes to define what a legal vote is and to mandate a manual recount implementing that definition. The recount mechanisms implemented in response to the deci-

Celluloid spinner button satirizing the problem of "chads" hanging from Florida ballots.

sions of the Florida Supreme Court do not satisfy the minimum requirement for non-arbitrary treatment of voters necessary to secure the fundamental right. Florida's basic command for the count of legally cast votes is to consider the "intent of the voter." *Gore v. Harris*, ___ So. 2d, at ___ (slip op., at 39). This is unobjectionable as an abstract proposition and a starting principle. The problem inheres in the absence of specific standards to ensure its equal application. The formulation of uniform rules to determine intent based on these recurring circumstances is practicable and, we conclude, necessary.

The law does not refrain from searching for the intent of the actor in a multitude of circumstances; and in some cases the general command to ascertain intent is not susceptible to much further refinement. In this instance, however, the question is not whether to believe a witness but how to interpret the marks or holes or scratches on an inanimate object, a piece of cardboard or paper which, it is said, might not have registered as a vote during the machine count. The factfinder confronts a thing, not a person. The search for intent can be confined by specific rules designed to ensure uniform treatment.

The want of those rules here has led to unequal evaluation of ballots in various respects. See *Gore v. Harris*, ___ So. 2d, at ___ (slip op., at 51) (Wells, J., dissenting) ("Should a county canvassing board count or not count a 'dimpled chad' where the voter is able to successfully dislodge the chad in every other contest on that ballot? Here, the county canvassing boards disagree"). As seems to have been acknowledged at oral argument, the standards for accepting or rejecting contested ballots might vary not only from county to county but indeed within a single county from one recount team to another.

The record provides some examples. A monitor in Miami-Dade County testified at trial that he observed that three members of the county canvassing board applied different standards in defining a legal vote. 3 Tr. 497, 499 (Dec. 3, 2000). And testimony at trial also revealed that at least one county changed its evaluative standards during the counting process. Palm Beach County, for example, began the process with a 1990 guideline which precluded counting completely attached chads, switched to a rule that considered a vote to be legal if any light could be seen through a chad, changed back to the 1990 rule, and then abandoned any pretense of a *per se* rule, only to have a court order that the county consider dimpled chads legal. This is not a process with sufficient guarantees of equal treatment.

An early case in our one person, one vote jurisprudence arose when a State accorded arbitrary and disparate treatment to voters in its different counties. *Gray v. Sanders*, 372 U.S. 368 (1963). The Court found a constitutional violation. We relied on these principles in the context of the Presidential selection process in *Moore v. Ogilvie*, 394 U.S. 814 (1969), where we invalidated a county-based procedure that diluted the influence of citizens in larger counties in the nominating process. There we observed that "[t]he idea that one group can be granted greater voting strength than another is hostile to the one man, one vote basis of our representative government." *Id.*, at 819.

The State Supreme Court ratified this uneven treatment. It mandated that the recount totals from two counties, Miami-Dade and Palm Beach, be included in the certified total. The court also appeared to hold *sub silentio* that the recount totals from Broward County, which were not completed until after the original November 14 certification by the Secretary of State, were to be considered part of the new certified vote totals even though the county certification was not contested by Vice President Gore. Yet each of the counties used varying standards to determine what was a legal vote. Broward County used a more forgiving standard than Palm Beach County, and uncovered almost three times as many new votes, a result markedly disproportionate to the difference in population between the counties.

In addition, the recounts in these three counties were not limited to so-called undervotes but extended to all of the ballots. The distinction has real consequences. A manual recount of all ballots identifies not only those ballots which show no vote but also those which contain more than one, the so-called overvotes. Neither category will be counted by the machine. This is not a trivial concern. At oral argument, respondents estimated there are as many as 110,000 overvotes statewide. As a result, the citizen whose ballot was not read by a machine because he failed to vote for a candidate in a way readable by a machine may still have his vote counted in a manual recount; on the other hand, the citizen who marks two candidates in a way discernable by the machine will not have the same opportunity to have his vote count, even if a manual examination of the ballot would reveal the requisite indicia of intent. Furthermore, the citizen who marks two candidates, only one of which is discernable by the machine, will have his vote counted even though it should have been read as an invalid ballot. The State Supreme Court's inclusion of vote counts based on these variant standards exemplifies concerns with the remedial processes that were under way.

That brings the analysis to yet a further equal protection problem. The votes certified by the court included a partial total from one county, Miami-Dade. The Florida Supreme Court's decision thus gives no assurance that the recounts included in a final certification must be complete. Indeed, it is respondent's submission that it would be consistent with the rules of the recount procedures to include whatever partial counts are done by the time of final certification, and we interpret the Florida Supreme Court's decision to permit this. See ____ So. 2d, at ____, n. 21 (slip op., at 37, n. 21) (noting "practical difficulties" may control outcome of election, but certifying partial Miami-Dade total nonetheless). This accommodation no doubt results from the truncated contest period established by the Florida Supreme Court in *Bush I*, at respondents' own urging. The press of time does not diminish the constitutional concern. A desire for speed is not a general excuse for ignoring equal protection guarantees.

In addition to these difficulties the actual process by which the votes were to be counted under the Florida Supreme Court's decision raises further concerns. That order did not specify who would recount the ballots. The county canvassing boards were forced to pull together ad hoc teams comprised of judges from various Circuits who had no previous training in handling and interpreting ballots. Furthermore, while others were permitted to observe, they were prohibited from objecting during the recount.

The recount process, in its features here described, is inconsistent with the minimum procedures necessary to protect the fundamental right of each voter in the special instance of a statewide recount under the authority of a single state judicial officer. Our consideration is limited to the present circumstances, for the problem of equal protection in election processes generally presents many complexities.

The question before the Court is not whether local entities, in the exercise of their expertise, may develop different systems for implementing elections. Instead, we are presented with a situation where a state court with the power to assure uniformity has ordered a statewide recount with minimal procedural safeguards. When a court orders a statewide remedy, there must be at least some assurance that the rudimentary requirements of equal treatment and fundamental fairness are satisfied.

Given the Court's assessment that the recount process underway was probably being conducted in an unconstitutional manner, the Court stayed the order directing the recount so it could hear this case and render an expedited decision. The contest provision, as it was mandated by the State Supreme Court, is not well calculated to sustain the confidence that all citizens must have in the outcome of elections. The State has not shown that its procedures include the necessary safeguards. The problem, for instance, of the estimated 110,000 overvotes has not been addressed, although Chief Justice Wells called attention to the concern in his dissenting opinion. See ____ So. 2d, at ____, n. 26 (slip op., at 45, n. 26).

Upon due consideration of the difficulties identified to this point, it is obvious that the recount cannot be conducted in compliance with the requirements of equal protection and due process without substantial additional work. It would require not only the adoption (after opportunity for argument)

Humorous rectangular celluloid button. The "for Dummies" books were a popular series that covered a variety of diverse topics, from personal finance to auto repair to golf.

of adequate statewide standards for determining what is a legal vote, and practicable procedures to implement them, but also orderly judicial review of any disputed matters that might arise. In addition, the Secretary of State has advised that the recount of only a portion of the ballots requires that the vote tabulation equipment be used to screen out undervotes, a function for which the machines were not designed. If a recount of overvotes were also required, perhaps even a second screening would be necessary. Use of the equipment for this purpose, and any new software developed for it, would have to be evaluated for accuracy by the Secretary of State, as required by Fla. Stat. §101.015 (2000).

The Supreme Court of Florida has said that the legislature intended the State's electors to "participat[e] fully in the federal electoral process," as provided in 3 U.S.C. § 5. ___ So. 2d, at ___ (slip op. at 27); see also *Palm Beach Canvassing Bd. v. Harris*, 2000 WL 1725434, *13 (Fla. 2000). That statute, in turn, requires that any controversy or contest that is designed to lead to a con-

Between December 2–4, 2000, before the Supreme Court decision which effectively ended the vote recount in Florida, the Gallup Poll conducted an exhaustive study of the public's view of media coverage of the presidential election. The findings showed that Americans were more likely than at any point in the previous fifteen years to say that news organizations' stories and reports are inaccurate. When respondents were given a choice, almost two-thirds said that news organizations' stories and reports are often inaccurate, while only one-third said that they get the facts straight. Additionally, about half perceived that there was a bias toward one political party or the other in the way these organizations reported the news; by a 2-to-1 margin, those who felt there was a bias said it favored Democrats.

This question has been asked by Gallup several times in the past dating back to 1985. The high points for perceptions of accurate news media coverage came in 1985 and 1989, when 55 percent and 54 percent, respectively, chose that alternative. Before the December 2000 poll, the low point came in August 1988, during a time of intense political coverage of the 1988 presidential race, when only 40 percent chose the "accurate" alternative. In 2000, 65 percent said that news coverage is often inaccurate; 32 percent said news organizations get the facts straight.

An election-night guest pass for the Democratic National Convention's party at Washington's Mayflower Hotel is pictured.

clusive selection of electors be completed by December 12. That date is upon us, and there is no recount procedure in place under the State Supreme Court's order that comports with minimal constitutional standards. Because it is evident that any recount seeking to meet the December 12 date will be unconstitutional for the reasons we have discussed, we reverse the judgment of the Supreme Court of Florida ordering a recount to proceed.

Seven Justices of the Court agree that there are constitutional problems with the recount ordered by the Florida Supreme Court that demand a remedy. See post, at 6 (Souter, J., dissenting); post, at 2, 15 (Breyer, J., dissenting). The only disagreement is as to the remedy. Because the Florida Supreme Court has said that the Florida Legislature intended to obtain the safe-harbor benefits of 3 U.S.C. § 5 Justice Breyer's proposed remedy—remanding to the Florida Supreme Court for its ordering of a constitutionally proper contest until December 18—contemplates action in violation of the Florida election code, and hence could not be part of an "appropriate" order authorized by Fla. Stat. §102.168(8) (2000).

* * *

None are more conscious of the vital limits on judicial authority than are the members of this Court, and none stand more in admiration of the Constitution's design to leave the selection of the President to the people, through their legislatures, and to the political sphere. When contending parties invoke the process of the courts, however, it becomes our unsought responsibility to resolve the federal and constitutional issues the judicial system has been forced to confront.

The judgment of the Supreme Court of Florida is reversed, and the case is remanded for further proceedings not inconsistent with this opinion.

Pursuant to this Court's Rule 45.2, the Clerk is directed to issue the mandate in this case forthwith.

It is so ordered.

Remarks by Gore and Bush on December 13, 2000

On December 13, Vice President Al Gore conceded the presidential election to Governor Bush. Very few countries settle contested political power so peacefully. Indeed, it is a tribute to the Founding Fathers and their genius in establishing a democracy. There were no riots, no troops in the streets. Rather, a Gallup Poll taken immediately after Gore's gracious speech showed that 83 percent of registered voters will accept Bush "as the legitimate president"—but with 84 percent of Gore voters maintaining that they did not consider themselves to be a Bush supporter.

Bush's first formal statement as president-elect tried to pull the nation together after its grueling ordeal. "I will be guided by President Jefferson's sense of purpose," stated Bush, "to stand for principle, to be reasonable in manner, and above all, to do great good for the cause of freedom and harmony." His excruciating close victory also marked the first time since 1955 that the Democratic Party did not control the White House or one congressional chamber.

Al Gore Televised Address, December 13, 2000

Good evening.

Just moments ago, I spoke with George W. Bush and congratulated him on becoming the 43rd president of the United States—and I promised him that I wouldn't call him back this time.

I offered to meet with him as soon as possible so that we can start to heal the divisions of the campaign and the contest through which we just passed.

Almost a century and a half ago, Senator Stephen Douglas told Abraham Lincoln, who had just defeated him for the presidency, "Partisan feeling must yield to patriotism. I'm with you, Mr. President, and God bless you."

Well, in that same spirit, I say to President-elect Bush that what remains of partisan rancor must now be put aside, and may God bless his stewardship of this country.

Neither he nor I anticipated this long and difficult road. Certainly neither of us wanted it to happen. Yet it came, and now it has ended, resolved, as it must be resolved, through the honored institutions of our democracy.

Over the library of one of our great law schools is inscribed the motto, "Not under man but under God and law." That's the ruling principle of American freedom, the source of our democratic liberties. I've tried to make it my guide throughout this contest as it has guided America's deliberations of all the complex issues of the past five weeks.

Now the U.S. Supreme Court has spoken. Let there be no doubt, while I strongly disagree with the court's decision, I accept it. I accept the finality of this outcome which will be ratified next Monday in the Electoral College. And tonight, for the sake of our unity of the people and the strength of our democracy, I offer my concession.

I also accept my responsibility, which I will discharge unconditionally, to honor the new president elect and do everything possible to help him bring Americans together in fulfillment of the great vision that our Declaration of Independence defines and that our Constitution affirms and defends.

Let me say how grateful I am to all those who supported me and supported the cause for which we have fought. Tipper and I feel a deep gratitude to Joe and Hadassah Lieberman who brought passion and high purpose to our partnership and opened new doors, not just for our campaign but for our country.

This has been an extraordinary election. But in one of God's unforeseen paths, this belatedly broken impasse can point us all to a new common ground, for its very closeness can serve to remind us that we are one people with a shared history and a shared destiny.

Indeed, that history gives us many examples of contests as hotly debated, as fiercely fought, with their own challenges to the popular will.

Other disputes have dragged on for weeks before reaching resolution. And each time, both the victor and the vanquished have accepted the result peacefully and in the spirit of reconciliation.

So let it be with us.

I know that many of my supporters are disappointed. I am too. But our disappointment must be overcome by our love of country.

And I say to our fellow members of the world community, let no one see this contest as a sign of American weakness. The strength of American democracy is shown most clearly through the difficulties it can overcome.

Some have expressed concern that the unusual nature of this election might hamper the next president in the conduct of his office. I do not believe it need be so.

President-elect Bush inherits a nation whose citizens will be ready to assist him in the conduct of his large responsibilities.

I personally will be at his disposal, and I call on all Americans—I particularly urge all who stood with us to unite behind our next president. This is

America. Just as we fight hard when the stakes are high, we close ranks and come together when the contest is done.

And while there will be time enough to debate our continuing differences, now is the time to recognize that that which unites us is greater than that which divides us.

While we yet hold and do not yield our opposing beliefs, there is a higher duty than the one we owe to political party. This is America and we put country before party. We will stand together behind our new president.

As for what I'll do next, I don't know the answer to that one yet. Like many of you, I'm looking forward to spending the holidays with family and old friends. I know I'll spend time in Tennessee and mend some fences, literally and figuratively.

Some have asked whether I have any regrets and I do have one regret: that I didn't get the chance to stay and fight for the American people over the next four years, especially for those who need burdens lifted and barriers removed, especially for those who feel their voices have not been heard. I heard you and I will not forget.

I've seen America in this campaign and I like what I see. It's worth fighting for—and that's a fight I'll never stop.

As for the battle that ends tonight, I do believe as my father once said, that no matter how hard the loss, defeat might serve as well as victory to shape the soul and let the glory out.

So for me this campaign ends as it began: with the love of Tipper and our family; with faith in God and in the country I have been so proud to serve, from Vietnam to the vice presidency; and with gratitude to our truly tireless campaign staff and volunteers, including all those who worked so hard in Florida for the last 36 days.

Now the political struggle is over and we turn again to the unending struggle for the common good of all Americans and for those multitudes around the world who look to us for leadership in the cause of freedom.

In the words of our great hymn, "America, America": "Let us crown thy good with brotherhood, from sea to shining sea."

And now, my friends, in a phrase I once addressed to others, it's time for me to go.

Thank you and good night, and God bless America.

George W. Bush Televised Address, December 13, 2000

[O]ur country has been through a long and trying period, with the outcome of the presidential election not finalized for longer than any of us could ever imagine.

Vice President Gore and I put our hearts and hopes into our campaigns. We both gave it our all. We shared similar emotions, so I understand how difficult this moment must be for Vice President Gore and his family.

He has a distinguished record of service to our country as a congressman, a senator and a vice president.

This evening I received a gracious call from the vice president. We agreed to meet early next week in Washington and we agreed to do our best to heal our country after this hard-fought contest.

Tonight I want to thank all the thousands of volunteers and campaign workers who worked so hard on my behalf.

I also salute the vice president and his supporters for waging a spirited campaign. And I thank him for a call that I know was difficult to make. Laura and I wish the vice president and Senator Lieberman and their families the very best.

I have a lot to be thankful for tonight. I'm thankful for America and thankful that we were able to resolve our electoral differences in a peaceful way.

I'm thankful to the American people for the great privilege of being able to serve as your next president.

I want to thank my wife and our daughters for their love. Laura's active involvement as first lady has made Texas a better place, and she will be a wonderful first lady of America.

I am proud to have Dick Cheney by my side, and America will be proud to have him as our next vice president.

Tonight I chose to speak from the chamber of the Texas House of Representatives because it has been a home to bipartisan cooperation. Here in a place where Democrats have the majority, Republicans and Democrats have worked together to do what is right for the people we represent.

We've had spirited disagreements. And in the end, we found constructive consensus. It is an experience I will always carry with me, an example I will always follow. [. . .]

The spirit of cooperation I have seen in this hall is what is needed in Washington, D.C. It is the challenge of our moment. After a difficult election, we must put politics behind us and work together to make the promise of America available for every one of our citizens.

I am optimistic that we can change the tone in Washington, D.C.

I believe things happen for a reason, and I hope the long wait of the last five weeks will heighten a desire to move beyond the bitterness and partisanship of the recent past.

Our nation must rise above a house divided. Americans share hopes and goals and values far more important than any political disagreements.

Republicans want the best for our nation, and so do Democrats. Our votes may differ, but not our hopes.

I know America wants reconciliation and unity. I know Americans want progress. And we must seize this moment and deliver.

Together, guided by a spirit of common sense, common courtesy, and common goals, we can unite and inspire the American citizens.

Together, we will work to make all our public schools excellent, teaching every student of every background and every accent, so that no child is left behind.

Together we will save Social Security and renew its promise of a secure retirement for generations to come.

Together we will strengthen Medicare and offer prescription drug coverage to all of our seniors.

Together we will give Americans the broad, fair and fiscally responsible tax relief they deserve.

Together we'll have a bipartisan foreign policy true to our values and true to our friends, and we will have a military equal to every challenge and superior to every adversary.

Together we will address some of society's deepest problems one person at a time, by encouraging and empowering the good hearts and good works of the American people.

This is the essence of compassionate conservatism and it will be a foundation of my administration.

These priorities are not merely Republican concerns or Democratic concerns; they are American responsibilities.

During the fall campaign, we differed about the details of these proposals, but there was remarkable consensus about the important issues before us: excellent schools, retirement and health security, tax relief, a strong military, a more civil society.

We have discussed our differences. Now it is time to find common ground and build consensus to make America a beacon of opportunity in the 21st century.

I'm optimistic this can happen. Our future demands it and our history proves it. Two hundred years ago, in the election of 1800, America faced another close presidential election. A tie in the Electoral College put the outcome into the hands of Congress.

After six days of voting and 36 ballots, the House of Representatives elected Thomas Jefferson the third president of the United States. That election brought the first transfer of power from one party to another in our new democracy.

Shortly after the election, Jefferson, in a letter titled "Reconciliation and

Reform," wrote this. "The steady character of our countrymen is a rock to which we may safely moor; unequivocal in principle, reasonable in manner. We should be able to hope to do a great deal of good to the cause of freedom and harmony."

Two hundred years have only strengthened the steady character of America. And so as we begin the work of healing our nation, tonight I call upon that character: respect for each other, respect for our differences, generosity of spirit, and a willingness to work hard and work together to solve any problem.

I have something else to ask you, to ask every American. I ask for you to pray for this great nation. I ask for your prayers for leaders from both parties. I thank you for your prayers for me and my family, and I ask you to pray for Vice President Gore and his family.

I have faith that with God's help we as a nation will move forward together as one nation, indivisible. And together we will create an America that is open, so every citizen has access to the American dream; an America that is educated, so every child has the keys to realize that dream; and an America that is united in our diversity and our shared American values that are larger than race or party.

I was not elected to serve one party, but to serve one nation.

The president of the United States is the president of every single American, of every race and every background.

Whether you voted for me or not, I will do my best to serve your interests and I will work to earn your respect.

I will be guided by President Jefferson's sense of purpose, to stand for principle, to be reasonable in manner, and above all, to do great good for the cause of freedom and harmony.

The presidency is more than an honor. It is more than an office. It is a charge to keep, and I will give it my all.

Thank you very much and God bless America.

Bush's Inaugural Address

On January 20, 2001, **George Walker Bush** took the oath of office on the same **Bible** used at his father's swearing-in, a 1767 King James Version also used when **George Washington** was inaugurated as the first president in 1789. With the new president on the stage before the **West Front of the Capitol** were the people who helped propel him to the presidency: his wife **Laura**, who supported him in finding discipline and purpose in his adult life; former president **George Bush**, who bequeathed to him a name and a network of political connections; **Bill Clinton**, whose personal scandals gave Bush a fighting chance against a sitting vice president; and that vice president, **Al Gore**, who ran what many political analysts thought to be a lackluster campaign. In addition, **Chief Justice William Rehnquist**, who administered the oath, had voted with the bare majority of the Supreme Court to effectively end Gore's legal contest of the returns from the polls in Florida. That decision determined the outcome of a breathtakingly close election.

As the new president pledged in his inaugural address to unify the nation, arguments persisted about the legitimacy of his victory. Thousands of the doubtful took to the streets of Washington in angry protest, the first substantial demonstration at an inauguration since **Richard Nixon's** second in 1973 during the **Vietnam War**.

President Clinton, distinguished guests and my fellow citizens, the peaceful transfer of authority is rare in history, yet common in our country. With a simple oath, we affirm old traditions and make new beginnings.

As I begin, I thank President Clinton for his service to our nation.

And I thank Vice President Gore for a contest conducted with spirit and ended with grace.

I am honored and humbled to stand here, where so many of America's leaders have come before me, and so many will follow.

We have a place, all of us, in a long story—a story we continue, but whose end we will not see. It is the story of a new world that became a friend and liberator of the old, a story of a slave holding society that became a servant of freedom, the story of a power that went into the world to protect but not possess, to defend but not to conquer.

It is the American story—a story of flawed and fallible people, united across the generations by grand and enduring ideals.

The grandest of these ideals is an unfolding American promise that everyone belongs, that everyone deserves a chance, that no insignificant person was ever born.

Americans are called to enact this promise in our lives and in our laws. And though our nation has sometimes halted, and sometimes delayed, we must follow no other course.

Through much of the last century, America's faith in freedom and democracy was a rock in a raging sea. Now it is a seed upon the wind, taking root in many nations.

Our democratic faith is more than the creed of our country, it is the inborn hope of our humanity, an ideal we carry but do not own, a trust we bear and pass along. And even after nearly 225 years, we have a long way yet to travel.

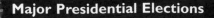

Postcards from the 2000 campaign in support of George W. Bush.

Dear Friend:

We need a leader who will listen to those who live off the land. That leader is George W. Bush.

He is committed to opening international markets to America's farm products. As Governor of the second biggest agricultural state, he knows producers are important to America's prosperity. He'll work with us to make American agriculture strong.

Governor Bush will fight to eliminate the death tax, so families can pass their life's work to their children and grandchildren.

I hope you join me in voting for George W. Bush, Tuesday, November 7. This will be a close race; please take your friends and family to the polls.

FROM:

Paid for by The Michigan Republican State Committee

PLACE
20¢
STAMP
HERE

TO:

Dear Friend:

George W. Bush is the strong leader with new ideas that America needs. As President, he will work to usher in an era of personal responsibility where people are held accountable for their actions.

He'll reform education through local control, high standards and strong accountability.

He'll strengthen Social Security and reform Medicare so all seniors have access to affordable prescription drugs.

Governor Bush will rebuild America's military and build a missile defense.

And he will devote half the surplus to Social Security, a quarter to essential spending and debt reduction, and a quarter for a tax cut for every taxpayer.

George W. Bush is a good man who will restore dignity and honor to the White House.

I hope you join me in voting for George W. Bush, Tuesday, November 7. This will be a close race; please take your friends and family to the polls.

FROM:

Paid for by The Michigan Republican State Committee

A Fresh Start For Farmers

While many of our citizens prosper, others doubt the promise, even the justice, of our own country. The ambitions of some Americans are limited by failing schools and hidden prejudice and the circumstances of their birth. And sometimes our differences run so deep, it seems we share a continent, but not a country.

We do not accept this, and we will not allow it. Our unity, our union, is the serious work of leaders and citizens in every generation. And this is my solemn pledge: I will work to build a single nation of justice and opportunity.

I know this is in our reach because we are guided by a power larger than ourselves who creates us equal in His image.

And we are confident in principles that unite and lead us onward.

America has never been united by blood or birth or soil. We are bound by ideals that move us beyond our backgrounds, lift us above our interests, and teach us what it means to be citizens. Every child must be taught these principles. Every citizen must uphold them. And every immigrant, by embracing these ideals, makes our country more, not less, American.

Today, we affirm a new commitment to live out our nation's promise through civility, courage, compassion and character.

America, at its best, matches a commitment to principle with a concern for civility. A civil society demands from each of us good will and respect, fair dealing and forgiveness.

Some seem to believe that our politics can afford to be petty because, in a time of peace, the stakes of our debates appear small.

But the stakes for America are never small. If our country does not lead the cause of freedom, it will not be led. If we do not turn the hearts of children toward knowledge and character, we will lose their gifts and undermine their idealism. If we permit our economy to drift and decline, the vulnerable will suffer most.

We must live up to the calling we share. Civility is not a tactic or a sentiment. It is the determined choice of trust over cynicism, of community over chaos. And this commitment, if we keep it, is a way to shared accomplishment.

America, at its best, is also courageous.

Our national courage has been clear in times of depression and war, when defending common dangers defined our common good. Now we must choose if the example of our fathers and mothers will inspire us or condemn us. We must show courage in a time of blessing by confronting problems instead of passing them on to future generations.

Together, we will reclaim America's schools, before ignorance and apathy claim more young lives.

We will reform Social Security and Medicare, sparing our children from struggles we have the power to prevent. And we will reduce taxes, to recover the momentum of our economy and reward the effort and enterprise of working Americans.

We will build our defenses beyond challenge, lest weakness invite challenge.

We will confront weapons of mass destruction, so that a new century is spared new horrors.

The enemies of liberty and our country should make no mistake: America remains engaged in the world by history and by choice, shaping a balance of power that favors freedom. We will defend our allies and our interests. We will show purpose without arrogance. We will meet aggression and bad faith with resolve and strength. And to all nations, we will speak for the values that gave our nation birth.

In the last days of July, Governor Bush surprised the nation by selecting Dick Cheney as his vice-presidential running mate. Choosing the former secretary of defense, 59 years of age, produced a range of lively editorial opinion as Cheney's extensive résumé also included several heart-related incidents, some requiring surgery. Cheney represented the political link between Bush and former President Bush, who himself lobbied for him. Much of the national commentary on the Republican ticket contrasted Cheney's extensive political experience with the more limited service of Bush. Their partisan foes chortled that they were two Texas oil men.

Celluloid Bush button.

America, at its best, is compassionate. In the quiet of American conscience, we know that deep, persistent poverty is unworthy of our nation's promise.

And whatever our views of its cause, we can agree that children at risk are not at fault. Abandonment and abuse are not acts of God, they are failures of love.

And the proliferation of prisons, however necessary, is no substitute for hope and order in our souls.

Where there is suffering, there is duty. Americans in need are not strangers, they are citizens, not problems, but priorities. And all of us are diminished when any are hopeless.

Government has great responsibilities for public safety and public health, for civil rights and common schools. Yet compassion is the work of a nation, not just a government.

And some needs and hurts are so deep they will only respond to a mentor's touch or a pastor's prayer. Church and charity, synagogue and mosque lend our communities their humanity, and they will have an honored place in our plans and in our laws.

Many in our country do not know the pain of poverty, but we can listen to those who do.

And I can pledge our nation to a goal: When we see that wounded traveler on the road to Jericho, we will not pass to the other side.

FIGHTING FOR ALL OUR FAMILIES

Al Gore upset political convention by choosing Senator Joseph I. Lieberman as his running mate. The Connecticut senator's national reputation rested on his moral edge, prominently displayed when, on the Senate floor, he criticized Bill Clinton's dalliances. Lieberman had associated himself with conspicuous, if ineffectual, efforts to decrease the degrading content of television and films. The loquacious Lieberman stood in the moderate center of the Democratic Party. As the first Jew to be on a national presidential ticket, he used this moment of emotional excitement by proclaiming his religious beliefs, thus inviting either tolerance or bigotry.

America, at its best, is a place where personal responsibility is valued and expected.

Encouraging responsibility is not a search for scapegoats, it is a call to conscience. And though it requires sacrifice, it brings a deeper fulfillment. We find the fullness of life not only in options, but in commitments. And we find that children and community are the commitments that set us free.

Our public interest depends on private character, on civic duty and family bonds and basic fairness, on uncounted, unhonored acts of decency which give direction to our freedom.

Sometimes in life we are called to do great things. But as a saint of our times has said, every day we are called to do small things with great love. The most important tasks of a democracy are done by everyone.

I will live and lead by these principles: to advance my convictions with civility, to pursue the public interest with courage, to speak for greater justice and compassion, to call for responsibility and try to live it as well.

In all these ways, I will bring the values of our history to the care of our times.

What you do is as important as anything government does. I ask you to seek a common good beyond your comfort; to defend needed reforms against easy attacks; to serve your nation, beginning with your neighbor. I ask you to be citizens: citizens, not spectators; citizens, not subjects; responsible citizens, building communities of service and a nation of character.

Americans are generous and strong and decent, not because we believe in ourselves, but because we hold beliefs beyond ourselves. When this spirit of citizenship is missing, no government program can replace it. When this spirit is present, no wrong can stand against it.

After the Declaration of Independence was signed, Virginia statesman John Page wrote to Thomas Jefferson: "We know the race is not to the swift nor the battle to the strong. Do you not think an angel rides in the whirlwind and directs this storm?"

Much time has passed since Jefferson arrived for his inauguration. The years and changes accumulate. But the themes of this day he would know: our nation's grand story of courage and its simple dream of dignity.

We are not this story's author, who fills time and eternity with his purpose. Yet his purpose is achieved in our duty, and our duty is fulfilled in service to one another.

Never tiring, never yielding, never finishing, we renew that purpose today, to make our country more just and generous, to affirm the dignity of our lives and every life.

This work continues. This story goes on. And an angel still rides in the whirlwind and directs this storm.

God bless you all, and God bless America.

Today, our fellow citizens, our way of life, our very freedom came under attack in a series of deliberate and deadly terrorist acts. The victims were in airplanes, or in their offices; secretaries, businessmen and women, military and federal workers; moms and dads, friends and neighbors. Thousands of lives were suddenly ended by evil, despicable acts of terror.

The pictures of airplanes flying into buildings, fires burning, huge structures collapsing, have filled us with disbelief, terrible sadness, and a quiet, unyielding anger. These acts of mass murder were intended to frighten our nation into chaos and retreat. But they have failed; our country is strong.

A great people has been moved to defend a great nation. Terrorist attacks can shake the foundations of our biggest buildings, but they cannot touch the foundation of America. These acts shattered steel, but they cannot dent the steel of American resolve.

America was targeted for attack because we're the brightest beacon for freedom and opportunity in the world. And no one will keep that light from shining.

Today, our nation saw evil, the very worst of human nature. And we responded with the best of America—with the daring of our rescue workers, with the caring for strangers and neighbors who came to give blood and help in any way they could.

Immediately following the first attack, I implemented our government's emergency response plans. Our military is powerful, and it's prepared. Our emergency teams are working in New York City and Washington, D.C. to help with local rescue efforts.

Our first priority is to get help to those who have been injured, and to take every precaution to protect our citizens at home and around the world from further attacks.

The functions of our government continue without interruption.

Federal agencies in Washington which had to be evacuated today are reopening for essential personnel tonight, and will be open for business tomorrow. Our financial institutions remain strong, and the American economy will be open for business, as well.

The search is underway for those who are behind these evil acts. I've directed the full resources of our intelligence and law enforcement communities to find those responsible and to bring them to justice. We will make no distinction between the terrorists who committed these acts and those who harbor them.

I appreciate so very much the members of Congress who have joined me in strongly condemning these attacks. And on behalf of the American people, I thank the many world leaders who have called to offer their condolences and assistance.

America and our friends and allies join with all those who want peace and security in the world, and we stand together to win the war against terrorism. Tonight, I ask for your prayers for all those who grieve, for the children whose worlds have been shattered, for all whose sense of safety and security has been threatened. And I pray they will be comforted by a power greater than any of us, spoken through the ages in Psalm 23: "Even though I walk through the valley of the shadow of death, I fear no evil, for You are with me."

This is a day when all Americans from every walk of life unite in our resolve for justice and peace. America has stood down enemies before, and we will do so this time. None of us will ever forget this day. Yet, we go forward to defend freedom and all that is good and just in our world.

Thank you. Good night, and God bless America.

On the evening of September 11, 2001, the Gallup Poll conducted a national survey of reaction to the terrorist attacks in which hijacked airplanes deliberately crashed into the twin towers of New York City's World Trade Center and into the Pentagon in Arlington, Virginia. Most Americans considered these events as an act of war (86 percent) and as the most tragic news event in their lifetimes (87 percent). They also were much more worried than they had been over the previous six years that someone in their own family would become a victim of a terrorist attack (58 percent), and a majority believed that the most recent attacks represented the beginning of a sustained terrorist campaign against the United States that would continue for weeks (55 percent).

Despite these views, respondents expressed a high level of confidence that the perpetrators would be identified and punished (88 percent), and expressed confidence in President Bush's ability to handle the situation (78 percent). They also resisted any call for immediate military strikes against known terrorist organizations (21 percent). Instead, they preferred that the United States take the time to clearly identify those who are responsible, even if it took months to do so, before conducting retaliatory strikes (71 percent).

The public's immediate reaction about the possible long-term effects of the terrorist attacks was mixed. About one-half thought that Americans would permanently change the way they live as a consequence of the attacks (49 percent), while the other half (45 percent) disagreed. Just over one-third (36 percent) thought they would make changes in their lives to reduce their chances of being a victim of a terrorist attack, but six in ten (61 percent) said they would not make any changes. Still, about one-half said that the events of September 11 made them less willing to fly on an airplane (48 percent).

This survey was completed before President Bush's September 11th evening speech to the nation. The results show a remarkable level of consensus among respondents about what the terrorist attacks meant and what the United States should do.

Reducing Nuclear Weapons

In November 2001, President Bush and Russian President Vladimir Putin met at Bush's ranch in Crawford, Texas, to discuss a variety of issues, including reduction of nuclear weapons and the existing Antiballistic Missile Treaty, established between the United States and the Soviet Union in 1972. On May 24, 2002, during Bush's visit to Moscow, the two world leaders signed the Moscow Treaty on Strategic Offensive Reductions. At the time the treaty was signed, the United States and Russia each had about 6,000 long-range, or strategic, nuclear weapons. The treaty calls for reducing this number to between 1,700 and 2,200 by the year 2012.

While the treaty was generally applauded, some felt it did not go far enough. Objections included the fact that the treaty did not include rules for verifying the reduction or a schedule to deactivate weapons; instead, it states only that the reduction goals be reached by 2012, the last year of the treaty. Also, the treaty has no provision for reducing the levels of short-range, or tactical, nuclear weapons. Finally, the treaty calls only for the weapons to be deactivated, not destroyed; they may be placed in storage and reactivated when either side feels it necessary.

Remarks by President Bush

President Putin, thank you very much. Laura and I are so grateful for your hospitality and your friendship. It's an historic and hopeful day for Russia and America. It's an historic day for the world, as well.

President Putin and I today ended a long chapter of confrontation, and opened up an entirely new relationship between our countries. Mr. President, I appreciate your leadership. I appreciate your vision. I appreciate the fact that we've now laid the foundation for not only our governments, but future governments to work in a spirit of cooperation and a spirit of trust. That's good. It's good for the people of Russia; it's good for the people of the United States.

President Putin and I have signed a treaty that will substantially reduce our nuclear—strategic nuclear warhead arsenals to the range of 1,700 to 2,200, the lowest level in decades. This treaty liquidates the Cold War legacy of nuclear hostility between our countries.

We've also signed a joint declaration of new strategic relationship that charts a course toward greater security, political and economic cooperation between Russia and the United States. Our nations will continue to cooperate closely in the war against global terror.

I understand full well that the people of Russia have suffered at the hands of terrorists. And so have we. And I want to thank President Putin for his understanding of the nature of the new war we face together, and his willingness to be determined and steadfast and patient as we pursue this war together.

President Putin and I agree also that the greatest danger in this war is the prospect of terrorists acquiring weapons of mass destruction. Our nations must spare no effort at preventing all forms of proliferation. And we discussed Iran in this context today. We'll work closely with each other on this very important issue.

Our nations also agree on the importance of a new NATO-Russia Council that will be launched in a few days in Rome. And, Mr. President, this council is also a tribute to your leadership and your vision. For decades, Russia and NATO were adversaries. Those days are gone, and that's good. And that's good for the Russian people, it's good for the people of my country, it's good for the people of Europe and it's good for the people of the world.

Russia and the United States are also determined to work closely on important regional challenges. Together, we will work to rebuild Afghanistan. Together, we will work to improve security in Georgia. We will work to help end fighting and achieve a political settlement in Chechnya.

Russia and the United States are committed to economic cooperation. We have launched a major new energy partnership. Private firms will take the lead in developing and transforming the vast energy reserves of Russia and the Caspian world to markets through multiple pipelines such as the Caspian Pipeline Consortium and Baku-Jihan. And I want to thank you for the cooperation and the willingness to work together on energy and energy security.

Russia is building its market economy, opening new opportunities for both our countries. I'm impressed by the level of entrepreneurial growth here in Russia. It's a significant achievement. Again, it's a testimony to the leadership of Vladimir Putin.

In a while, we're going to meet with Russian and American business leaders to discuss how we can continue fostering good relations and fostering opportunity. We want Russia to be a part of the world economy. We look forward to one day welcoming Russia as a member of the World Trade Organization. President Putin and I also agree that we'll work to resolve disputed areas of trading, such as poultry or steel, in a spirit of mutual respect and trust.

America welcomes the dramatic improvement in freedoms in Russia since Soviet days, including the new freedoms of Russia's Jewish community. In recognition of these freedoms, I am determined to work with Congress to remove Russia from the Jackson-Vanik amendment. It is time our Congress responded to my request, President Putin's desire, that the Jackson-Vanik amendment be removed pertaining to Russia.

I also discussed with President Putin the important role of free press in building a working democracy. And today we will meet with media entrepreneurs from both countries. It's an issue we discussed before. The President said it makes sense to have a forum where media entrepreneurs can meet and visit. And it's going to take place today. Mr. President, I appreciate that.

I am pleased with our relationship. I am confident that by working together, we make the world more peaceful. I'm confident that by working together, we can win the first war of the 21st century, and that is the war [. . .] against cold-blooded killers, who want to harm nations such as America and Russia. And I'm confident that when we work together in a spirit of cooperation on all fronts, both our peoples will benefit.

Mr. President, thank you for your hospitality.

Remarks by President Putin

Distinguished American colleagues, and distinguished Mr. President, ladies and gentlemen. We've just accomplished the official part of our talks with U.S. President George Bush, for our distinguished colleagues of the visit in Moscow and St. Petersburg, but now we can name the major result of our talks—first of all, the logical development and practical implementation as seen by our agreements reached in Crawford last year. I mean the signature of the treaty between Russia on strategic defensive reductions and, first of all, this document.

It's the statement of our countries to reduce our nuclear arsenals and the joint work for nonproliferation of weapons of mass destruction. It's the decision of two states which are particularly responsible for international security and strategic stability. We're on the level of adopting the declaration on new strategic relationship which determines the basic directions in the security and international policy.

It will have a positive impact for economic cooperation and development of our relations between the institutions of general public, and together with Mr. President, we discussed especially this aspect, the civil society between the people of our countries. The declaration formulates the principles of our dialogue, anti-missile dialogue. That is the transparency and openness and exclusion of potential threats. We confirmed the Genoa agreement on offensive and defensive systems in all their aspects.

A separate issue, the mechanism of NATO-Russia cooperation within the framework of 20, it presumes a new level of joint responsibility and confidence between all its participants.

I would like to stress especially that is the international novelty. And it happened because of the strengthening of Russian-American relations, including in joint confrontation to international terrorists struggling with international terrorism. [. . .] The memory of terrorism victims and the responsibility for the security of our people means joint struggle against this evil, as well as the struggle against Nazism. The spirit of our cooperation will mean fruitful results even today.

That's why the agenda has very concrete issues of interaction against terrorism on the basis of unique standards against any manifestation of terrorism and extremism. We need close contacts through all agencies and services, including special services. Here we have very positive experience we've accrued over the past years. And we see today—we feel it today during the negotiations.

The bilateral working group on Afghanistan has demonstrated its efficiency. And we, Mr. President, would like to transform it on a group to combat terrorism, especially chemical, biological, nuclear terrorism.

Russia and the United States are oriented to build new relations in economic activity. Our businessman mentality is much alike, that their qualities and their joint work is based on free trade and supporting the initiatives.

That's why our task is to open new opportunities for business community.

We need to avoid obstacles of the past. Here we mean not only the market status of the Russian economy—and I'm grateful to Mr. President that he has given a very positive signal during our talks. And it does also mean such things as Jackson-Vanik amendment; we have to remove administrative obstacles, which encurls both countries to cooperate, especially in the high-tech sphere, which determined the economy of the 21st century—that is the aeronautics, telecommunications, science and technologies, new sources of energy. I would like to focus on energy, especially nuclear energy. We paid much attention to it today. And the large format of our cooperation will be a great element for the global economy on the whole.

I would like to stress, in conclusion, that, of course, not all ideas, not all initiatives, are on paper and in the form of official documents. But a serious move forward in all these issues is quite evident for us. Today we together counteract global threats and challenges and we're going to form a stable world order that is within the interests of our peoples and our countries. And I think it's in the interest of all the civilized human society.

Presidents Bush and Putin respond to questions

Reporter: I have a question for both Presidents, please. If we've truly entered a new era, why do you each need 1,700 nuclear weapons? And, President Putin, why does Russia need to continue producing nuclear warheads? And to, President Bush, why does the United States need to keep some 2,000 of these weapons in storage, ready for deployment?

Bush: First of all, remember where we've come from. We've come from 6,000 to 1,700 in a very quick—or to 1,700 to 2,200 in a very quick period of time. You know, friends really don't need weapons pointed at each other. We both understand that. But it's a realistic assessment of where we've been. And who knows what will happen 10 years from now. Who knows what future presidents will say and how they react.

If you have a nuclear arsenal, you want to make sure they work. It's—one reason that you keep weapons in storage apart from launchers is for quality control. And the thing I think it's important for you to know, Ron, is that we've made tremendous progress from the past. And the treaty is setting a period of time in the rear-view mirror of both countries. And I am not only confident that this is good for world peace, I'm confident this sets the stage for incredible cooperation that we've never had before between our countries.

Putin: I concur with the assessment given by my colleague, Mr. Bush. And naturally, our position is well-known, we are guided by the facts that it's more worthwhile perhaps to eliminate a certain part of nuclear potentials. At the same time, I'd like to point out another thing here. Any man who has at least once in his career dealt with arms, had arms in his hands, at least to hunt or a rifle or whatever, he knows that it's much better, much safer to have it in stock disarmed, disassembled perhaps, rather than to have it in your arms and charged with bullets in it and with your finger on the trigger at the same time. This is a different state of affairs, as it were.

And the fact that we agreed with President Bush regarding such detente, in such manner, this is a serious move ahead to ensure international security, which is a very good sign as regards the relationship between our two countries.

Now, as to why Russia should continue to produce nuclear arms, I'd like to say that this is not our priority. But in addition to Russia and U.S. out there, there are other states who possess nuclear arms. What is more concerning, there are countries who want to acquire weapons of mass destruction. Experts in the area of international security are aware of the fact, and they have been talking a lot about nuclear arms as deterrent.

Moreover, many of them assert—and it is difficult to dispute this fact—they say the existence of the nuclear arms was an impediment, an obstacle which contained the world from large-scale wars over the past decades, let's say. And I think we should take that into consideration while building a new quality of relationship within the two main nuclear states of the world.

Between August 18–19, 2000, the Gallup Poll asked registered voters: "Regardless of which presidential candidate you support, please tell me if you think Al Gore or George W. Bush would better handle each of the following issues." On the issue of abortion, 48 percent felt Gore would handle the issue better, compared to 36 percent for Bush. In contrast, on the issue of handling "national defense," Bush received 54 percent to 38 percent for Gore.

In a Gallup Poll conducted July 9–11, 2002, Bush's overall job approval rating stood at 69 percent, the first time the president's approval had fallen below 70 percent in the 10-plus months since September 11. The last president to maintain a 70 percent or higher rating for 10 or more months was Lyndon B. Johnson (1963–64)

We also should pay attention to the whole set of relations currently in the world out there and we should take into account the prospects of development of the world in the realm of security, bearing in mind those potential threats I've mentioned here.

Reporter: Mr. Bush, when we can hope that Jackson-Vanik will be rescinded, which currently is very out of place? That's, you know, a remnant of the Cold War here. And will the U.S.—can you use it as a leverage of applying pressure on Russia? And when Russia will finally be recognized as a marketplace country? And what's the prospect of Russia's accession to WTO?

And now to Mr. Putin, Russian President. What's your idea of how U.S. Boeings can help Russian civil aviation?

Bush: I couldn't make myself clearer during my opening statement about how I feel about Jackson-Vanik—not much action by the Congress of the United States and I hope they act. The market-based economy is an issue that the President and I talked about. It is a regulatory matter, the responsibility of which resides at the Commerce Department. Secretary Evans and I have to talk about this subject, and we'll have an answer to the President soon.

And in terms of success of Russia ascending into the WTO, it's something that we want. It's in our nation's interest that Russia be a part of the WTO. And we look forward to working with the President and respective ministers, to see that that happens. It's in our interest that that happen. So it's hard for me to predict the timetables on all the issues you mentioned. Those over which I have got direct control will happen relatively quickly.

Putin: Well, you know, while talking about the whole set of commercial and trade ties between our two countries, today we've mentioned more than once that we are facing somewhat an unusual situation in this area today, which has to do with the fact that while improving relations in disarmament matters, building confidence and so on and so forth, at the same time, we're expanding the whole set of relations in economic area. And, naturally, we'll face new problems we never had to deal with before.

The position taken by the U.S. administration and the President is known to us as regards Jackson-Vanik. It's precisely the administration who initiated its rescinding. And business communities of our two countries, American and Russian business communities,and their interaction together with the interaction of the parliamentary issues, will be able to remove similar problems in automatic manner, I guess.

Now, as regards your specific question on purchase of Boeings, I must say that the best lobbyist of the interests of U.S. companies will be American President standing here, since both Boeings and poultry and other matters very often have been told by my colleagues. People usually say, well, it's not on our level, but I must say—and then there will be a lengthy monologue on specific matters.

Anyhow, you've posed a very acute and very specific question. Why it's acute, because it's on the agenda or practical interaction. And it's very specific since it has a bearing to very specific matters. And since it's acute and specific, I'll answer as one should in gentlemen's society, in a very general manner.

First and foremost, our carriers, in my opinion, should be primarily guided towards Russian aircraft producers. Why? Because Russian manufacturers, you know, don't have anywhere to sell their products, otherwise, because they are not let anywhere, or with a lot of difficulty. They only can sell it domestically. That's the first thing. And here we can talk about interaction on the market. Now, the second thing, primarily Aeroflot, should be competitive on the market, and should have advanced technology in their hands. Therefore, they both have American Boeings today. They also have European Airbus aircraft. And the question has been raised currently on additional purchase, on replacement of old equipment with those foreign aircraft.

Now, I should say, depending on the decision to be taken by economic structures, this is not a political question, mind you. The economic structure should decide on it. A lot will depend on it in regards of the state of our political interaction, of course. And our American colleague's proposal today is a little bit costlier than the European's proposal. Had Americans bought our cheap aluminum and steel, then their aircraft would have been cheaper and more competitive, including in our market.

So all of this jointly has been a subject of our discussions with the President here, and our good friend and partner, Secretary of Commerce and economy. And I think that in the course of normalization of trade and commerce relations, all these issues will be addressed in a most mutually advantageous manner.

Reporter: State sponsorship of terrorism—I wonder because of that if these Russians sales that you object to continue, does this new strategic relationship you're discussing today bump up against what you outlined in your speech to Congress when you said, in the war against terrorism, you're either with the United States or against the United States?

And, President Putin, the Bush team says that your sales of nuclear technology and sophisticated military technology to Iran are the world's single biggest proliferation problem right now. Do you agree with that assessment, and did you make any specific promises today in your meeting with President Bush?

Bush: Well, first, we spent a lot of time on this subject. And as I said yesterday in Germany, I worry about Iran and I'm confident Vladimir Putin worries about Iran, and that was confirmed today. He understands terrorist threats, just like we understand terrorist threats. And he understands that weapons of mass destruction are dangerous to Russia, just as they are to America. And he's explained that point himself, of course. [. . .]

But we spoke very frankly and honestly about the need to make sure that a non-transparent government run by radical clerics doesn't get their hands on weapons of mass destruction. It could be harmful to us and harmful to Russia. And the President can speak for himself. And he gave me some assurances that I think will be very comforting for you to listen to. And I'm confident we can work together on this issue. This is in both our countries' mutual interest that we solve this problem.

Putin: I will confirm what Mr. Bush has just said, and I agree with your evaluation of threats in this regard. Generally speaking, I believe that the problem of nonproliferation is one of the key problems as regards ensuring international security.

Incidentally, this happened to be one of the main motivating and underpinning logical stimuluses to work in Russia-NATO framework together on non-proliferation on nuclear arms.

At the same time, I'd like to point out that cooperation between Iran and Russia is not all a character which would undermine the process on non-proliferation. Our cooperation is exclusively, as regards the energy sector, focused on the problems of economic nature. I'd like to point out also that the U.S. has taken a commitment upon themselves to build similar nuclear power plant in North Korea, similar to Russia.

And in addition to Iran, I think, we also need to think about other countries here. For example, we have some questions concerning development of missile programs in Taiwan, in some other countries where we've been witnessing active work of producing mass destruction weapons and their carriers. All of that should be a subject of our in-depth discussion both bilaterally and in the frameworks of NATO-Russia agreement. That's one of the key issues of the modern times, I believe.

It would seem to me that in order to be efficient, in this sense, like in other areas, we need to address the main task, to upgrade confidence mutually. And today I mentioned to President Bush here, that as regards Iran and some other countries, according to our data, the missile programs of those countries, nuclear programs, are built largely on the basis of the technologies and with the support of the Western companies. We do have such info, and we stand ready to share it with our American partners. So if we pursued that way, not dealing with generalities, then we'll get results with respect to this very complicated and very important for our two countries track.

And the conclusive question.

Reporter: To both Presidents, to what extent the treaty ensures real nuclear parity, and are there conditions that the treaty can be terminated by either side? And how true is the fact that Russia still remains as one of the nuclear targets for nuclear forces? And how does that relate to the announced new strategic relations between our two countries?

Bush: This document is a treaty that will be confirmed by the United States Senate and the Duma, hopefully.

Secondly, treaties have always had outs; there's nothing new about that. There are conditions of which things may change and people get out of treaties. That's the way it's been. The Antiballistic Missile Treaty had an out; there's nothing new about that. And, thirdly, you know, we are going to work to end the—forever end the Cold War. And that begins with the statement that Russia's our friend, not our enemy.

And you say targeting—I mean, the idea of our weaponry, our military has no aims at Russia. There may be old vestiges in place, but Russia's not an

In December 2001, President Bush indicated that in six months the United States would withdraw from the Antiballistic Missile (ABM) Treaty it had signed with the Soviet Union in 1972. Bush explained that continued participation in the treaty would prevent the United States from developing a national missile defense (NMD) system that would protect American cities from attack by nuclear missiles launched by "rogue states" like Iraq, Iran, and North Korea. This decision was made despite opposition from Russia and China, as well as U.S. allies.

An initial response from Russian lawmakers was to increase production of antiballistic nuclear weapons to pre-1972 levels. This possibility was eliminated with the May 2002 Moscow Treaty.

The "Strategic Defense Initiative" concept had originated nearly 20 years earlier, during the Reagan administration. Supporters argued that such a system, which would use ground-based rockets to shoot down enemy missiles before they reached their targets, would eliminate the possibility of nuclear war. Though it received little notice in the press, in February 2002 a ship-based anti-missile system was tested successfully.

Opponents note the complexity of building a system able to destroy enemy missiles in flight—sometimes compared to "hitting a bullet with a bullet." They also argue that deployment will exacerbate, not reduce, the threat from China, Russia, and other nuclear powers. They point out that in September 2000, President Clinton said, "I simply cannot conclude with the information I have today that we have enough confidence in the technology, and the operational effectiveness of the entire NMD system, to move forward to deployment." Finally, they note that terrorists or rogue states would be unlikely to launch nuclear missiles; a more frightening scenario is that of a terrorist bomb hidden in a suitcase or the trunk of a car parked in a major city—a potential attack from which the National Missile Defense system would offer no defense.

By the summer of 2002, when the United States officially abrogated the ABM Treaty, there were an estimated 31,000 nuclear warheads stockpiled by eight nations: the United States, Russia, the United Kingdom, France, China, Israel, India, and Pakistan. France has no missile delivery system, while Israel, India, and Pakistan have missiles with ranges of less than 1,300 miles (2,000 km).

enemy. You don't think about how to deal with Russia the way they used to. Russia is a friend. And that's the new thinking. That's part of what's being codified today.

Putin: As regards the parity, the parity relationship of sorts, the weight of military potentials and nuclear potential, and so on, so forth, each state would have its own strategy of development of what you refer to as nuclear deterrent process. But I'd like to assure you that all the action undertaken by us in this area fully confirmed with the interests of the Russian Federation. The documents signed today are a result of joint effort of the Minister of Defense and Chiefs of staff and our Minister of Foreign Affairs, of course, jointly with our American colleagues. And we proceed from the assumption we have today, and we try to forecast the status of affairs in the world for a lengthy period of time—I would like to point out, again, for a lengthy perspective.

Now, as regards the question of verification and control, perhaps, I'd like to point out that we're very much satisfied with the U.S. administration approach to this question. Our American partners have agreed that we need to retain START I, which is provided for by the system of verification. We agreed we will continue this work on the basis of the documents signed today, as well. [. . .]

Thank you. Thank you for your kind attention and for your participation.

On New Palestinian Leadership

Throughout 2001 and into 2002, mounting violence between Palestinians and Israelis dominated news headlines. The Gallup Poll found the public decidedly pessimistic about long-term chances of peace in the Middle East—with about two-thirds saying "there will not come a time when Israel and Arab nations will be able to settle their differences and live in peace." The Bush administration continued to take an active role in attempting to find a diplomatic solution to the violence.

In August 2001, the Gallup Poll showed by little more than a 3-to-1 margin (41 percent to 13 percent) Americans said their sympathies were more with the Israelis than with the Palestinian Arabs in the Middle East situation. That left close to one-half (46 percent) who indicated no preference between the two sides, 7 percent who said their sympathies were with both sides equally, 18 percent whose sympathies were with neither side, and 21 percent who had no opinion on the matter.

For too long, the citizens of the Middle East have lived in the midst of death and fear. The hatred of a few holds the hopes of many hostage. The forces of extremism and terror are attempting to kill progress and peace by killing the innocent. And this casts a dark shadow over an entire region. For the sake of all humanity, things must change in the Middle East.

It is untenable for Israeli citizens to live in terror. It is untenable for Palestinians to live in squalor and occupation. And the current situation offers no prospect that life will improve. Israeli citizens will continue to be victimized by terrorists, and so Israel will continue to defend herself.

In the situation the Palestinian people will grow more and more miserable. My vision is two states, living side by side in peace and security. There is simply no way to achieve that peace until all parties fight terror. Yet, at this critical moment, if all parties will break with the past and set out on a new path, we can overcome the darkness with the light of hope. Peace requires a new and different Palestinian leadership, so that a Palestinian state can be born.

I call on the Palestinian people to elect new leaders, leaders not compromised by terror. I call upon them to build a practicing democracy, based on tolerance and liberty. If the Palestinian people actively pursue these goals, America and the world will actively support their efforts. If the Palestinian people meet these goals, they will be able to reach agreement with Israel and Egypt and Jordan on security and other arrangements for independence.

And when the Palestinian people have new leaders, new institutions and new security arrangements with their neighbors, the United States of America will support the creation of a Palestinian state whose borders and certain aspects of its sovereignty will be provisional until resolved as part of a final settlement in the Middle East.

In the work ahead, we all have responsibilities. The Palestinian people are gifted and capable, and I am confident they can achieve a new birth for their nation. A Palestinian state will never be created by terror—it will be built through reform. And reform must be more than cosmetic change, or veiled attempt to preserve the status quo. True reform will require entirely new political and economic institutions, based on democracy, market economics and action against terrorism.

Today, the elected Palestinian legislature has no authority, and power is concentrated in the hands of an unaccountable few. A Palestinian state can

During the late 19th century, a movement to establish a nation in Palestine as a homeland for Jews gained momentum. After World War I, the region was controlled by Great Britain; the Balfour Declaration (1917) had asserted support for the creation of a Jewish state, and Jewish immigration to the region increased, along with violence between Palestine's Jewish and Arab communities. After World War II and the murder of 6 million Jews in Nazi-controlled Europe, international support for a Jewish state led in 1947 to a United Nations plan to divide Palestine into separate Jewish and Arab states.

In May 1948, Great Britain pulled out of Palestine and the State of Israel was proclaimed. The new state was immediately invaded by its Arab neighbors—Egypt, Syria, Jordan, Iraq, Saudi Arabia and Lebanon. However, Israel's army withstood this attack, and its War of Independence ended in 1949 with Israel gaining some 2,500 square miles of territory. Jordan occupied the West Bank (territory along the Jordan River and Dead Sea which it annexed in 1950) and Egypt occupied the Gaza Strip (a region on the eastern Mediterranean). During and after the 1948 war, some 800,000 Arabs left Palestine, living in exile in the neighboring Arab countries. In 1967, when Israel again fought the Arab states in what became known as the Six Day War, Israel gained control of the West Bank and Gaza Strip. Hundreds of thousands of Palestinian Arabs left their homes; many remained in the occupied territories, living under Israeli control.

Throughout the 1970s and 1980s, various Palestinian groups fought to recover their lands, often stating the destruction of Israel as their goal. The most well-known of these groups, the Palestine Liberation Organization only serve its citizens with a new constitution which separates the powers of government. The Palestinian parliament should have the full authority of a legislative body. Local officials and government ministers need authority of their own and the independence to govern effectively.

The United States, along with the European Union and Arab states, will work with Palestinian leaders to create a new constitutional framework, and a working democracy for the Palestinian people. And the United States, along with others in the international community will help the Palestinians organ-

---

(PLO), was run by Yasser Arafat and his Fatah movement, which had started terrorist attacks against Israeli targets in the mid-1960s. In 1982 Israel invaded Lebanon, where the PLO was based, in an attempt to eliminate the organization. The controversial war increased international sympathy for the Palestinian cause; however, much goodwill was lost after the 1985 *Achille Lauro* affair, in which PLO terrorists hijacked a cruise ship, shot a wheelchair-bound Jewish passenger, and dumped his body overboard.

By 1988, Arafat had publicly renounced terrorism and acknowledged the right of Israel to exist as a state. In 1993, talks in Norway between representatives of Israel and the PLO led to the Oslo Accords, which set a timetable for Israeli withdrawal from the occupied territories and established the eventual possibility of an independent Palestinian state. Over the next six years, additional agreements were signed between Israel and Arafat's group (now called the Palestinian Authority, and considered by Israel the official representative of the Palestinians). In July 2000, Israeli Prime Minister Ehud Barak and Arafat met with President Bill Clinton at Camp David, for intensive negotiations for a final status agreement. On July 25, Clinton announced that the summit had failed—no agreement had been reached. In the fall of 2000, a new wave of violence broke out in the region, making further negotiation all but impossible.

The Palestinian-Israeli violence continued through the first two years of President Bush's term with no sign of abating. By June 2002, when Bush made his statement on the Palestinian leadership, hundreds of Israelis and Palestinians had been killed.

ize and monitor fair, multi-party local elections by the end of the year, with national elections to follow.

Today, the Palestinian people live in economic stagnation, made worse by official corruption. A Palestinian state will require a vibrant economy, where honest enterprise is encouraged by honest government. The United States, the international donor community and the World Bank stand ready to work with Palestinians on a major project of economic reform and development. The United States, the EU, the World Bank, the International Monetary Fund are willing to oversee reforms in Palestinian finances, encouraging transparency and independent auditing.

And the United States, along with our partners in the developed world, will increase our humanitarian assistance to relieve Palestinian suffering. Today, the Palestinian people lack effective courts of law and have no means to defend and vindicate their rights. A Palestinian state will require a system of reliable justice to punish those who prey on the innocent. The United States and members of the international community stand ready to work with Palestinian leaders to establish finance—establish finance and monitor a truly independent judiciary.

Today, Palestinian authorities are encouraging, not opposing, terrorism. This is unacceptable. And the United States will not support the establishment of a Palestinian state until its leaders engage in a sustained fight against the terrorists and dismantle their infrastructure. This will require an externally supervised effort to rebuild and reform the Palestinian security services. The security system must have clear lines of authority and accountability and a unified chain of command.

America is pursuing this reform along with key regional states. The world is prepared to help, yet ultimately these steps toward statehood depend on the Palestinian people and their leaders. If they energetically take the path of reform, the rewards can come quickly. If Palestinians embrace democracy, confront corruption and firmly reject terror, they can count on American support for the creation of a provisional state of Palestine.

With a dedicated effort, this state could rise rapidly, as it comes to terms with Israel, Egypt, and Jordan on practical issues, such as security. The final borders, the capital and other aspects of this state's sovereignty will be negotiated between the parties, as part of a final settlement. Arab states have offered their help in this process, and their help is needed.

I've said in the past that nations are either with us or against us in the war on terror. To be counted on the side of peace, nations must act. Every leader actually committed to peace will end incitement to violence in official media, and publicly denounce homicide bombings. Every nation actually committed to peace will stop the flow of money, equipment and recruits to terrorist groups seeking the destruction of Israel—including Hamas, Islamic Jihad, and Hezbollah. Every nation actually committed to peace must block the shipment of Iranian supplies to these groups, and oppose regimes that promote terror, like Iraq. And Syria must choose the right side in the war on terror by closing terrorist camps and expelling terrorist organizations.

Leaders who want to be included in the peace process must show by their deeds an undivided support for peace. And as we move toward a peaceful solution, Arab states will be expected to build closer ties of diplomacy and commerce with Israel, leading to full normalization of relations between Israel and the entire Arab world.

Israel also has a large stake in the success of a democratic Palestine. Permanent occupation threatens Israel's identity and democracy. A stable, peaceful Palestinian state is necessary to achieve the security that Israel longs for. So I challenge Israel to take concrete steps to support the emergence of a viable, credible Palestinian state.

As we make progress towards security, Israeli forces need to withdraw fully to positions they held prior to September 28, 2000. And consistent with the recommendations of the Mitchell Committee, Israeli settlement activity in the occupied territories must stop.

The Palestinian economy must be allowed to develop. As violence subsides, freedom of movement should be restored, permitting innocent Palestinians to resume work and normal life. Palestinian legislators and officials, humanitarian and international workers, must be allowed to go about the business of building a better future. And Israel should release frozen Palestinian revenues into honest, accountable hands.

I've asked Secretary Powell to work intensively with Middle Eastern and international leaders to realize the vision of a Palestinian state, focusing them on a comprehensive plan to support Palestinian reform and institution-building.

Ultimately, Israelis and Palestinians must address the core issues that divide them if there is to be a real peace, resolving all claims and ending the conflict between them. This means that the Israeli occupation that began in 1967 will be ended through a settlement negotiated between the parties, based on U.N. Resolutions 242 and 338, with Israeli withdrawal to secure and recognize borders.

We must also resolve questions concerning Jerusalem, the plight and future of Palestinian refugees, and a final peace between Israel and Lebanon, and Israel and a Syria that supports peace and fights terror.

All who are familiar with the history of the Middle East realize that there may be setbacks in this process. Trained and determined killers, as we have seen, want to stop it. Yet the Egyptian and Jordanian peace treaties with Israel remind us that with determined and responsible leadership progress can come quickly.

As new Palestinian institutions and new leaders emerge, demonstrating real performance on security and reform, I expect Israel to respond and work toward a final status agreement. With intensive effort by all, this agreement could be reached within three years from now. And I and my country will actively lead toward that goal.

I can understand the deep anger and anguish of the Israeli people. You've lived too long with fear and funerals, having to avoid markets and public transportation, and forced to put armed guards in kindergarten classrooms. The Palestinian Authority has rejected your offer at hand, and trafficked with terrorists. You have a right to a normal life; you have a right to security; and I deeply believe that you need a reformed, responsible Palestinian partner to achieve that security.

I can understand the deep anger and despair of the Palestinian people. For decades you've been treated as pawns in the Middle East conflict. Your interests have been held hostage to a comprehensive peace agreement that never seems to come, as your lives get worse year by year. You deserve democracy and the rule of law. You deserve an open society and a thriving economy. You deserve a life of hope for your children. An end to occupation and a peaceful democratic Palestinian state may seem distant, but America and our partners throughout the world stand ready to help, help you make them possible as soon as possible.

If liberty can blossom in the rocky soil of the West Bank and Gaza, it will inspire millions of men and women around the globe who are equally weary of poverty and oppression, equally entitled to the benefits of democratic government.

I have a hope for the people of Muslim countries. Your commitments to morality, and learning, and tolerance led to great historical achievements. And those values are alive in the Islamic world today. You have a rich culture, and you share the aspirations of men and women in every culture. Prosperity and freedom and dignity are not just American hopes, or Western hopes. They are universal, human hopes. And even in the violence and turmoil of the Middle East, America believes those hopes have the power to transform lives and nations.

This moment is both an opportunity and a test for all parties in the Middle East: an opportunity to lay the foundations for future peace; a test to show who is serious about peace and who is not. The choice here is stark and simple. The Bible says, "I have set before you life and death; therefore, choose life." The time has arrived for everyone in this conflict to choose peace, and hope, and life.

★ Bush's Homeland Security Strategy ★

On July 16, 2002, President Bush released his administration's National Strategy for Homeland Security.
This lengthy document detailed how the United
States would protect itself from domestic terrorism—
attacks such as those which occurred on September
11, 2001, or those involving chemical, biological (such
as anthrax), or nuclear weapons. In his comments
introducing the strategy in the White House Rose
Garden, Bush said, "All of us agree that protecting
Americans from attack is our most urgent national
priority, and that we must act on the priority." The
executive summary of the strategy, which provides an
overview of the 90-page document, is reprinted here.

This document is the first National Strategy for Homeland Security. The purpose of the Strategy is to mobilize and organize our Nation to secure the U.S. homeland from terrorist attacks. This is an exceedingly complex mission that requires coordinated and focused effort from our entire society—the federal government, state and local governments[1], the private sector, and the American people.

People and organizations all across the United States have taken many steps to improve our security since the September 11 attacks, but a great deal of work remains. The *National Strategy for Homeland Security* will help to prepare our Nation for the work ahead in several ways. It provides direction to the federal government departments and agencies that have a role in homeland security. It suggests steps that state and local governments, private companies and organizations, and individual Americans can take to improve our security and offers incentives for them to do so. It recommends certain actions to the Congress. In this way, the *Strategy* provides a framework for the contributions that we all can make to secure our homeland.

The *National Strategy for Homeland Security* is the beginning of what will be a long struggle to protect our Nation from terrorism. It establishes a foundation upon which to organize our efforts and provides initial guidance to prioritize the work ahead. The *Strategy* will be adjusted and amended over time. We must be prepared to adapt as our enemies in the war on terrorism alter their means of attack.

Strategic Objectives

The strategic objectives of homeland security in order of priority are to:

- Prevent terrorist attacks within the United States;
- Reduce America's vulnerability to terrorism; and
- Minimize the damage and recover from attacks that do occur.

Threat and Vulnerability

Unless we act to prevent it, a new wave of terrorism, potentially involving the world's most destructive weapons, looms in America's future. It is a challenge as formidable as any ever faced by our Nation. But we are not daunted. We possess the determination and the resources to defeat our enemies and secure our homeland against the threats they pose.

One fact dominates all homeland security threat assessments: terrorists are strategic actors. They choose their targets deliberately based on the weaknesses they observe in our defenses and our preparedness. We must defend ourselves against a wide range of means and methods of attack. Our enemies are working to obtain chemical, biological, radiological, and nuclear weapons for the purpose of wreaking unprecedented damage on America. Terrorists continue to employ conventional means of attack, while at the same time gaining expertise in less traditional means, such as cyber attacks. Our society presents an almost infinite array of potential targets that can be attacked through a variety of methods.

---

[1]The National Strategy for Homeland Security defines "State" to mean "any state of the United States, the District of Columbia, Puerto Rico, the Virgin Islands, Guam, American Samoa, the Canal Zone, the Commonwealth of the Northern Mariana Islands, or the trust territory of the Pacific Islands." The Strategy defines "local government" as "any county, city, village, town, district, or other political subdivision of any state, any Native American tribe or authorized tribal organization, or Alaska native village or organization, and includes any rural community or unincorporated town or village or any other public entity for which an application for assistance is made by a state or political subdivision thereof."

꒰ꖛ꒰ꖛ꒰ꖛ

[2]The distribution of the National Strategy for Homeland Security coincides with Congress' consideration of the President's proposal to establish a Department of Homeland Security. The Strategy refers to a "Department of Homeland Security" only to provide the strategic vision for the proposed Department and not to assume any one part of the President's proposal will or will not be signed into law.

Our enemies seek to remain invisible, lurking in the shadows. We are actively engaged in uncovering them. Al-Qaeda remains America's most immediate and serious threat despite our success in disrupting its network in Afghanistan and elsewhere. Other international terrorist organizations, as well as domestic terrorist groups, possess the will and capability to attack the United States.

Organizing for a Secure Homeland

In response to the homeland security challenge facing us, the President has proposed, and the Congress is presently considering, the most extensive reorganization of the federal government in the past fifty years. The establishment of a new Department of Homeland Security would ensure greater accountability over critical homeland security missions and unity of purpose among the agencies responsible for them.[2]

American democracy is rooted in the precepts of federalism—a system of government in which our state governments share power with federal institutions. Our structure of overlapping federal, state, and local governance—our country has more than 87,000 different jurisdictions—provides unique opportunity and challenges for our homeland security efforts. The opportunity comes from the expertise and commitment of local agencies and organizations involved in homeland security. The challenge is to develop interconnected and complementary systems that are reinforcing rather than duplicative and that ensure essential requirements are met. A national strategy requires a national effort.

State and local governments have critical roles to play in homeland security. Indeed, the closest relationship the average citizen has with government is at the local level. State and local levels of government have primary responsibility for funding, preparing, and operating the emergency services that would respond in the event of a terrorist attack. Local units are the first to respond, and the last to leave the scene. All disasters are ultimately local events.

The private sector—the Nation's principal provider of goods and services and owner of 85 percent of our infrastructure—is a key homeland security partner. It has a wealth of information that is important to the task of protecting the United States from terrorism. Its creative genius will develop the information systems, vaccines, detection devices, and other technologies and innovations that will secure our homeland.

An informed and proactive citizenry is an invaluable asset for our country in times of war and peace. Volunteers enhance community coordination and action, whether at the national or local level. This coordination will prove critical as we work to build the communication and delivery systems indispensable to our national effort to detect, prevent, and, if need be, respond to terrorist attack.

Critical Mission Areas

The *National Strategy for Homeland Security* aligns and focuses homeland security functions into six critical mission areas: intelligence and warning, border and transportation security, domestic counterterrorism, protecting critical infrastructure, defending against catastrophic terrorism, and emergency preparedness and response. The first three mission areas focus primarily on preventing terrorist attacks; the next two on reducing our Nation's vulnerabilities; and the final one on minimizing the damage and recovering from attacks that do occur. The *Strategy* provides a framework to align the resources of the federal budget directly to the task of securing the homeland.

Intelligence and Warning. Terrorism depends on surprise. With it, a terrorist attack has the potential to do massive damage to an unwitting and unprepared target. Without it, the terrorists stand a good chance of being preempted by authorities, and even if they are not, the damage that results from their attacks is likely to be less severe. The United States will take every necessary action to avoid being surprised by another terrorist attack. We must have an intelligence and warning system that can detect terrorist activity before it manifests itself in an attack so that proper preemptive, preventive, and protective action can be taken.

The *National Strategy for Homeland Security* identifies five major initiatives in this area:

- Enhance the analytic capabilities of the FBI;
- Build new capabilities through the Information Analysis and Infrastructure Protection Division of the proposed Department of Homeland Security;
- Implement the Homeland Security Advisory System;
- Utilize dual-use analysis to prevent attacks; and
- Employ "red team" techniques.

Border and Transportation Security. America historically has relied heavily on two vast oceans and two friendly neighbors for border security, and on the private sector for most forms of domestic transportation security. The increasing mobility and destructive potential of modern terrorism has required the United States to rethink and renovate fundamentally its systems for border and transportation security. Indeed, we must now begin to conceive of border security and transportation security as fully integrated requirements because our domestic transportation systems are inextricably intertwined with the global transport infrastructure. Virtually every community in America is connected to the global transportation network by the seaports, airports, highways, pipelines, railroads, and waterways that move people and goods into, within, and out of the Nation. We must therefore promote the efficient and reliable flow of people, goods, and services across borders, while preventing terrorists from using transportation conveyances or systems to deliver implements of destruction.

The *National Strategy for Homeland Security* identifies six major initiatives in this area:

- Ensure accountability in border and transportation security;
- Create "smart borders";
- Increase the security of international shipping containers;
- Implement the Aviation and Transportation Security Act of 2001;

- Recapitalize the U.S. Coast Guard; and
- Reform immigration services.

The President proposed to Congress that the principal border and transportation security agencies—the Immigration and Naturalization Service, the U.S. Customs Service, the U.S. Coast Guard, the Animal and Plant Health Inspection Service, and the Transportation Security Agency—be transferred to the new Department of Homeland Security. This organizational reform will greatly assist in the implementation of all the above initiatives.

Domestic Counterterrorism. The attacks of September 11 and the catastrophic loss of life and property that resulted have redefined the mission of federal, state, and local law enforcement authorities. While law enforcement agencies will continue to investigate and prosecute criminal activity, they should now assign priority to preventing and interdicting terrorist activity within the United States. The Nation's state and local law enforcement officers will be critical in this effort. Our Nation will use all legal means—both traditional and nontraditional—to identify, halt, and, where appropriate, prosecute terrorists in the United States. We will pursue not only the individuals directly involved in terrorist activity but also their sources of support: the people and organizations that knowingly fund the terrorists and those that provide them with logistical assistance.

Effectively reorienting law enforcement organizations to focus on counterterrorism objectives requires decisive action in a number of areas. The *National Strategy for Homeland Security* identifies six major initiatives in this area:
- Improve intergovernmental law enforcement coordination;
- Facilitate apprehension of potential terrorists;
- Continue ongoing investigations and prosecutions;
- Complete FBI restructuring to emphasize prevention of terrorist attacks;
- Target and attack terrorist financing; and
- Track foreign terrorists and bring them to justice.

Protecting Critical Infrastructure and Key Assets. Our society and modern way of life are dependent on networks of infrastructure—both physical networks such as our energy and transportation systems and virtual networks such as the Internet. If terrorists attack one or more pieces of our critical infrastructure, they may disrupt entire systems and cause significant damage to the Nation. We must therefore improve protection of the individual pieces and interconnecting systems that make up our critical infrastructure. Protecting America's critical infrastructure and key assets will not only make us more secure from terrorist attack, but will also reduce our vulnerability to natural disasters, organized crime, and computer hackers.

America's critical infrastructure encompasses a large number of sectors. The U.S. government will seek to deny terrorists the opportunity to inflict lasting harm to our Nation by protecting the assets, systems, and functions vital to our national security, governance, public health and safety, economy, and national morale.

The *National Strategy for Homeland Security* identifies eight major initiatives in this area:

- Unify America's infrastructure protection effort in the Department of Homeland Security;
- Build and maintain a complete and accurate assessment of America's critical infrastructure and key assets;
- Enable effective partnership with state and local governments and the private sector;
- Develop a national infrastructure protection plan;
- Secure cyberspace;
- Harness the best analytic and modeling tools to develop effective protective solutions;
- Guard America's critical infrastructure and key assets against "inside" threats; and
- Partner with the international community to protect our transnational infrastructure.

Defending against Catastrophic Threats. The expertise, technology, and material needed to build the most deadly weapons known to mankind—including chemical, biological, radiological, and nuclear weapons—are spreading inexorably. If our enemies acquire these weapons, they are likely to try to use them. The consequences of such an attack could be far more devastating than those we suffered on September 11—a chemical, biological, radiological, or nuclear terrorist attack in the United States could cause large numbers of casualties, mass psychological disruption, contamination and significant economic damage, and could overwhelm local medical capabilities.

Currently, chemical, biological, radiological, and nuclear detection capabilities are modest and response capabilities are dispersed throughout the country at every level of government. While current arrangements have proven adequate for a variety of natural disasters and even the September 11 attacks, the threat of terrorist attacks using chemical, biological, radiological, and nuclear weapons requires new approaches, a focused strategy, and a new organization.

The *National Strategy for Homeland Security* identifies six major initiatives in this area:

- Prevent terrorist use of nuclear weapons through better sensors and procedures;
- Detect chemical and biological materials and attacks;
- Improve chemical sensors and decontamination techniques;
- Develop broad spectrum vaccines, antimicrobials, and antidotes;
- Harness the scientific knowledge and tools to counter terrorism; and
- Implement the Select Agent Program.

Emergency Preparedness and Response. We must prepare to minimize the damage and recover from any future terrorist attacks that may occur despite our best efforts at prevention. An effective response to a major terrorist incident—as well as a natural disaster—depends on being prepared. Therefore, we need a comprehensive national system to bring together and coordinate all necessary response assets quickly and effectively. We must plan, equip, train, and exercise many different response units to mobilize without warning for any emergency.

Many pieces of this national emergency response system are already in place. America's first line of defense in the aftermath of any terrorist attack is its first responder community—police officers, firefighters, emergency medical providers, public works personnel, and emergency management officials. Nearly three million state and local first responders regularly put their lives on the line to save the lives of others and make our country safer.

Yet multiple plans currently govern the federal government's support of first responders during an incident of national significance. These plans and the government's overarching policy for counterterrorism are based on an artificial and unnecessary distinction between "crisis management" and "consequence management." Under the President's proposal, the Department of Homeland Security will consolidate federal response plans and build a national system for incident management in cooperation with state and local government. Our federal, state, and local governments would ensure that all response personnel and organizations are properly equipped, trained, and exercised to respond to all terrorist threats and attacks in the United States. Our emergency preparedness and response efforts would also engage the private sector and the American people.

The *National Strategy for Homeland Security* identifies twelve major initiatives in this area:
- Integrate separate federal response plans into a single all-discipline incident management plan;
- Create a national incident management system;
- Improve tactical counterterrorist capabilities;
- Enable seamless communication among all responders;
- Prepare health care providers for catastrophic terrorism;
- Augment America's pharmaceutical and vaccine stockpiles;
- Prepare for chemical, biological, radiological, and nuclear decontamination;
- Plan for military support to civil authorities;
- Build the Citizen Corps;

- Implement the First Responder Initiative of the Fiscal Year 2003 Budget;
- Build a national training and evaluation system; and
- Enhance the victim support system.

The Foundations of Homeland Security

The *National Strategy for Homeland Security* also describes four foundations—unique American strengths that cut across all of the mission areas, across all levels of government, and across all sectors of our society. These foundations—law, science and technology, information sharing and systems, and international cooperation—provide a useful framework for evaluating our homeland security investments across the federal government.

Law. Throughout our Nation's history, we have used laws to promote and safeguard our security and our liberty. The law will both provide mechanisms for the government to act and will define the appropriate limits of action.

The *National Strategy for Homeland Security* outlines legislative actions that would help enable our country to fight the war on terrorism more effectively. New federal laws should not preempt state law unnecessarily or overly federalize the war on terrorism. We should guard scrupulously against incursions on our freedoms.

The *Strategy* identifies twelve major initiatives in this area:
Federal level

- Enable critical infrastructure information sharing;
- Streamline information sharing among intelligence and law enforcement agencies;
- Expand existing extradition authorities;
- Review authority for military assistance in domestic security;
- Revive the President's reorganization authority; and
- Provide substantial management flexibility for the Department of Homeland Security.

State level

- Coordinate suggested minimum standards for state driver's licenses;
- Enhance market capacity for terrorism insurance;
- Train for prevention of cyber attacks;
- Suppress money laundering;
- Ensure continuity of the judiciary; and
- Review quarantine authorities.

Science and Technology. The Nation's advantage in science and technology is a key to securing the homeland. New technologies for analysis, information sharing, detection of attacks, and countering chemical, biological, radiological, and nuclear weapons will help prevent and minimize the damage from future terrorist attacks. Just as science has helped us defeat past enemies overseas, so too will it help us defeat the efforts of terrorists to attack our homeland and disrupt our way of life.

The federal government is launching a systematic national effort to harness science and technology in support of homeland security. We will build a national research and development enterprise for homeland security sufficient to mitigate the risk posed by modern terrorism. The federal government will consolidate most federally funded homeland security research and development under the Department of Homeland Security to ensure strategic direction and avoid duplicative efforts. We will create and implement a long-term research and development plan that includes investment in revolutionary capabilities with high payoff potential. The federal government will also seek to harness the energy and ingenuity of the private sector to develop and produce the devices and systems needed for homeland security.

The *National Strategy for Homeland Security* identifies eleven major initiatives in this area:

- Develop chemical, biological, radiological, and nuclear countermeasures;
- Develop systems for detecting hostile intent;
- Apply biometric technology to identification devices;

- Improve the technical capabilities of first responders;
- Coordinate research and development of the homeland security apparatus;
- Establish a national laboratory for homeland security;
- Solicit independent and private analysis for science and technology research;
- Establish a mechanism for rapidly producing prototypes;
- Conduct demonstrations and pilot deployments;
- Set standards for homeland security technology; and
- Establish a system for high-risk, high-payoff homeland security research.

Information Sharing and Systems. Information systems contribute to every aspect of homeland security. Although American information technology is the most advanced in the world, our country's information systems have not adequately supported the homeland security mission. Databases used for federal law enforcement, immigration, intelligence, public health surveillance, and emergency management have not been connected in ways that allow us to comprehend where information gaps or redundancies exist. In addition, there are deficiencies in the communications systems used by states and municipalities throughout the country; most state and local first responders do not use compatible communications equipment. To secure the homeland better, we must link the vast amounts of knowledge residing within each government agency while ensuring adequate privacy.

The *National Strategy for Homeland Security* identifies five major initiatives in this area:
- Integrate information sharing across the federal government;
- Integrate information sharing across state and local governments, private industry, and citizens;
- Adopt common "meta-data" standards for electronic information relevant to homeland security;
- Improve public safety emergency communications; and
- Ensure reliable public health information.

International Cooperation. In a world where the terrorist threat pays no respect to traditional boundaries, our strategy for homeland security cannot stop at our borders. America must pursue a sustained, steadfast, and systematic international agenda to counter the global terrorist threat and improve our homeland security. Our international anti-terrorism campaign has made significant progress since September 11. The full scope of these activities will be further described in the forthcoming National Security *Strategy* of the United States and the National *Strategy* for Combating Terrorism. The *National Strategy for Homeland Security* identifies nine major initiatives in this area:

- Create "smart borders";
- Combat fraudulent travel documents;
- Increase the security of international shipping containers;
- Intensify international law enforcement cooperation;
- Help foreign nations fight terrorism;
- Expand protection of transnational critical infrastructure;
- Amplify international cooperation on homeland security science and technology;
- Improve cooperation in response to attacks; and
- Review obligations to international treaties and law.

Costs of Homeland Security

The national effort to enhance homeland security will yield tremendous benefits and entail substantial financial and other costs. Benefits include reductions in the risk of attack and their potential consequences. Costs include not only the resources we commit to homeland security but also the delays to commerce and travel. The United States spends roughly $100 billion per year on homeland security. This figure includes federal, state, and local law enforcement and emergency services, but excludes most funding for the armed forces.

The responsibility of providing homeland security is shared between federal, state and local governments, and the private sector. In many cases, sufficient incentives exist in the private market to supply protection.

Government should fund only those homeland security activities that are not supplied, or are inadequately supplied, in the market. Cost sharing between different levels of government should reflect the principles of federalism. Many homeland security activities, such as intelligence gathering and border security, are properly accomplished at the federal level. In other circumstances, such as with first responder capabilities, it is more appropriate for state and local governments to handle these responsibilities.

Conclusion: Priorities for the Future

The *National Strategy for Homeland Security* sets a broad and complex agenda for the United States. The *Strategy* has defined many different goals that need to be met, programs that need to be implemented, and responsibilities that need to be fulfilled. But creating a strategy is, in many respects, about setting priorities—about recognizing that some actions are more critical or more urgent than others.

The President's Fiscal Year 2003 Budget proposal, released in February 2002, identified four priority areas for additional resources and attention in the upcoming year:

- Support first responders;
- Defend against bioterrorism;
- Secure America's borders; and
- Use 21st-century technology to secure the homeland.

Work has already begun on the President's Fiscal Year 2004 Budget. Assuming the Congress passes legislation to implement the President's proposal to create the Department of Homeland Security, the Fiscal Year 2004 Budget will fully reflect the reformed organization of the executive branch for homeland security. That budget will have an integrated and simplified structure based on the six critical mission areas defined by the *Strategy*. Furthermore, at the time the *National Strategy for Homeland Security* was published, it was expected that the Fiscal Year 2004 Budget would attach priority to the following specific items for substantial support:

- Enhance the analytic capabilities of the FBI;
- Build new capabilities through the Information Analysis and Infrastructure Protection Division of the proposed Department of Homeland Security;
- Create "smart borders"
- Improve the security of international shipping containers;
- Recapitalize the U.S. Coast Guard;
- Prevent terrorist use of nuclear weapons through better sensors and procedures;
- Develop broad spectrum vaccines, antimicrobials, and antidotes; and
- Integrate information sharing across the federal government.

In the intervening months, the executive branch will prepare detailed implementation plans for these and many other initiatives contained within the *National Strategy for Homeland Security*. These plans will ensure that the taxpayers' money is spent only in a manner that achieves specific objectives with clear performance-based measures of effectiveness.

Bush Signs Trade Bill

During and after the 2000 campaign, one of George Bush's policy goals was the passage of trade promotion authority, also known as fast track trade authority. This is legislation allowing the executive branch to negotiate trade agreements and open markets with other governments, which will be honored if approved by Congress. The original fast track legislation was passed during the Nixon administration and extended through 1994, when Congress allowed the authority to expire. Although President Bill Clinton pushed for new fast track legislation throughout his term, the Republican Congress refused to grant him the trade authority. In July 2002, Congress passed a trade bill that restored the fast track authority to the president, and George W. Bush signed it into law on August 6. Following are his remarks on signing the bill.

According to the White House, by the summer of 2002 there were some 190 preferential trade agreements worldwide, with the United States party to only three. In his remarks Bush indicated that he intended to use the fast track authority to negotiate better access for American exports.

During the years fast track authority was in effect (1974–1994), it was invoked only five times, most notably in negotiating the North American Free Trade Agreement (NAFTA) in 1993.

Thank you all very much for that warm welcome. Welcome to the people's house, as we celebrate a victory for the American economy. Last week, the United States Congress passed trade promotion authority and renewed an expanded the Andean Trade Preference Act.

Trade is an important source of good jobs for our workers and a source of higher growth for our economy. Trade is an important source of earnings for our farmers and for our factories. It creates new opportunities for our entrepreneurs. Trade expands choices for America's consumers and raises living standards for our families. And now, after eight years, America is back in the business of promoting open trade to build our prosperity and to spur economic growth. [. . .]

With trade promotion authority, the trade agreements I negotiate will have an up-or-down vote in Congress, giving other countries the confidence to negotiate with us. Five Presidents before me had this advantage, but since the authority elapsed in 1994, other nations and regions have pursued new trade agreements while America's trade policy was stuck in park.

With each passing day, America has lost trading opportunities, and the jobs and earnings that go with them. Starting now, America is back at the bargaining table in full force.

I will use trade promotion authority aggressively to create more good jobs for American workers, more exports for American farmers, and higher living standards for American families. Free trade has a proven track record for spurring growth and advancing opportunity for our working families.

Exports accounted for roughly one-quarter of all U.S. economic growth in the 1990s. Jobs in exporting plants pay wages that are up to 18 percent higher than jobs in non-exporting plants. And our two major trade agreements, NAFTA and the Uruguay Round, have created more choices and lower prices for consumers, while raising standards of living for the typical American family of four by $2,000 a year.

America will build on this record of success. A completely free global market for agricultural products, for example, would result in gains of as much as $13 billion a year for American farmers and consumers. Lowering global trade barriers on all products and services by even one-third could boost the U.S. economy by $177 billion a year, and raise living standards for the average family by $2,500 annually.

In other words, trade is good for the American people. And I'm going to use the trade promotion authority to bring these benefits to the American people.

Free trade is also a proven strategy for building global prosperity and adding to the momentum of political freedom. Trade is an engine of economic growth. It uses the power of markets to meet the needs of the poor. In our lifetime, trade has helped lift millions of people, and whole nations, and entire regions, out of poverty and put them on the path to prosperity.

History shows that as nations become more prosperous, their citizens will demand, and can afford, a cleaner environment. And greater freedom for commerce across the borders eventually leads to greater freedom for citizens within the borders.

The members of the diplomatic corps with us today understand the importance of free trade to their nations' success. They understand that trade is an enemy of poverty, and a friend of liberty. I want to thank the ambassadors for their role in getting this bill passed, especially the Andean ambassadors who are such strong advocates for the Andean Trade Preference Act. By providing trade preference for products from four Andean democracies, we will build prosperity, reduce poverty, strengthen democracy, and fight illegal drugs with expanding economic opportunity.

Trade promotion authority gives the United States an important tool to break down trade barriers with all countries. We'll move quickly to build free trade relationships with individual nations, such as Chile and Singapore and

Morocco. We'll explore free trade relationships with others, such as Australia. The United States will negotiate a Free Trade Area of the Americas, and pursue regional agreements with the nations of Central America and the Southern Africa Customs Union.

We'll move forward globally, working with all nations to make the negotiations begun last year in Doha a success. A little more than a week ago, the United States put forward a far-reaching proposal to lower worldwide agricultural trade barriers. These innovative set of ideas can lead to real progress in this challenging area.

Trade gives all nations the hope of sharing in the great economic, and social, and political progress of our age. And trade will give American workers the hope that comes from better and higher-paying jobs.

America's committed to building a world that trades in freedom and grows in prosperity and liberty. Today, we have the tools to pursue that vision, and I look forward to the work ahead.

Further Reading

GENERAL REFERENCE

Israel, Fred L. *Student's Atlas of American Presidential Elections, 1789–1996*. Washington, D.C.: Congressional Quarterly Books, 1998.

Levy, Peter B., editor. *100 Key Documents in American History*. Westport, Conn.: Praeger, 1999.

Mieczkowski, Yarek. *The Routledge Historical Atlas of Presidential Elections*. New York: Routledge, 2001.

Polsby, Nelson W., and Aaron Wildavsky. *Presidential Elections: Strategies and Structures of American Politics*. 10th edition. New York: Chatham House, 2000.

Watts, J. F., and Fred L. Israel, editors. *Presidential Documents*. New York: Routledge, 2000.

Widmer, Ted. *The New York Times Campaigns: A Century of Presidential Races*. New York: DK Publishing, 2000.

POLITICAL AMERICANA REFERENCE

Cunningham, Noble E. Jr. *Popular Images of the Presidency: From Washington to Lincoln*. Columbia: University of Missouri Press, 1991.

Melder, Keith. *Hail to the Candidate: Presidential Campaigns from Banners to Broadcasts*. Washington, D.C.: Smithsonian Institution Press, 1992.

Schlesinger, Arthur M. jr., Fred L. Israel, and David J. Frent. *Running for President: The Candidates and their Images*. 2 vols. New York: Simon and Schuster, 1994.

Warda, Mark. *100 Years of Political Campaign Collectibles*. Clearwater, Fla.: Galt Press, 1996.

THE ELECTION OF 2000
and the Administration of George W. Bush

Bush, George W. *A Charge to Keep: My Journey to the White House*. New York: HarperCollins, 1999.

Dershowitz, Alan M. *Supreme Injustice: How the High Court Hijacked Election 2000*. New York: Oxford University Press, 2001.

Gillman, Howard. *The Votes that Counted: How the Court Decided the 2000 Presidential Election*. Chicago: University of Chicago Press, 2001.

Gormley, Beatrice. *President George W. Bush: Our Forty-third President*. New York: Aladdin Paperbacks, 2001.

Kaplan, David A. *The Accidental President: How 413 Lawyers, 9 Supreme Court Justices, and 5,963,110 Floridians (Give or Take a Few) Landed George W. Bush in the White House*. New York: William Morrow and Company, 2001.

Minutaglio, Bill. *First Son and the Bush Family Dynasty*. New York: Random House, 1999.

Mitchell, Elizabeth. *Revenge of the Bush Dynasty*. New York: Hyperion, 2000.

Nader, Ralph. *Crashing the Party: How to Tell the Truth and Still Run for President*. New York: St. Martin's Press, 2002.

Posner, Richard A. *Breaking the Deadlock: The 2000 Election, the Constitution, and the Courts*. Princeton: Princeton University Press, 2001.

Rakove, Jack N., editor. *The Unfinished Election of 2000: Leading Scholars Examine America's Strangest Election*. New York: Basic Books, 2001.

Sammon, Bill. *At Any Cost: How Al Gore Tried to Steal the Election*. Washington, D.C.: Regnery Publishing, 2001.

Toobin, Jeffrey. *Too Close to Call: The Thirty-Six-Day Battle to Decide the 2000 Election*. New York: Random House, 2001.

INDEX

Numbers in **bold italics** refer to captions.

The EDITORS

ARTHUR M. SCHLESINGER JR. holds the Albert Schweitzer Chair in the Humanities at the Graduate Center of the City University of New York. He is the author of more than a dozen books, including *The Age of Jackson; The Vital Center; The Age of Roosevelt* (3 vols.); *A Thousand Days: John F. Kennedy in the White House; Robert Kennedy and His Times; The Cycles of American History;* and *The Imperial Presidency.* Professor Schlesinger served as Special Assistant to President Kennedy (1961–63). His numerous awards include: the Pulitzer Prize for History; the Pulitzer Prize for Biography; two National Book Awards; The Bancroft Prize; and the American Academy of Arts and Letters Gold Medal for History.

FRED L. ISRAEL is professor emeritus of American history, City College of New York. He is the author of *Nevada's Key Pittman* and has edited *The War Diary of Breckinridge Long* and *Major Peace Treaties of Modern History, 1648–1975* (5 vols.) He holds the Scribe's Award from the American Bar Association for his joint editorship of the *Justices of the United States Supreme Court* (4 vols.). For more than 25 years Professor Israel has compiled and edited the Gallup Poll into annual reference volumes.

JONATHAN H. MANN was eleven years old when he discovered his lifelong passion. His mother returned from a flea market with two campaign buttons—one for Thomas E. Dewey and one for Woodrow Wilson—and he has been intrigued with political Americana ever since. He graduated with a degree in history from Vassar College and holds an MBA from the Graduate School of Business Administration at New York University. Mr. Mann is the Executive Director of a non-profit consulting firm in New York City and he manages his own television production company. He also is the publisher of *The Rail Splitter—A Journal for the Lincoln Collector.*